M000112362

Endorsements for *Beyond Sight*

What's your idea of "a good read?" Inspirational? Travelogue? Memoir? You've come to the right place! Gayle Sommerfeld's Beyond Sight *shares her journey—literal and spiritual—as co-founder of MOST (Mission Opportunities Short Term) Ministries with her husband, Don.*

> **B.J. Connor**, writer for *Chicken Soup for the Soul* books, *Guideposts, Focus on the Family* and an Amy Foundation Writing Award winner.

Inspiring, thought-provoking, faith-building—this well-written memoir is a page-turner and certainly a story that will encourage you to follow God's leading in your own life. Gayle and Sandra invite us to join them on a spirit journey to discover how God works through real people to serve those who need us most. Expect a blessing! Highest recommendation for Beyond Sight*!*

> **Ruth N. Koch**, MA, NCC author of *Grace Notes*, co-author of *Speaking the Truth in Love*

If you've felt the Spirit's call to reach out to the poor and disadvantaged; if you've experienced a call from God to missions of any kind; if you've felt within your heart the desire to say, "Here I am. Send me;" Beyond Sight *is a must-read! You'll be touched by the powerful hand of God, who uses ordinary people to do extraordinary things. This book will give you courage to follow that still small voice.*

> **David Granner**, co-founder Bethania Kids, India

Beyond Sight *is a real page turner. You will wonder "What is God going to do next? How will He solve the next challenge?" as Gayle brings you into each mission country. You will come away in awe of God's creativity!*

> **Roxanne M. Smith**, author of *Struck Down, but Not Destroyed.*

Appreciation from the Mission Field

I have worked with many organizations and groups in organizing teams and activities. Simply put—working with MOST Ministries is one of the most organized and easy experiences I have ever had.

> Sean Harlow, missionary in **Asia**

MOST Ministries has it right! I was very much up front with the team that many short term mission trips are doing damage to mission fields, but that we trusted MOST was going to have it right. It could not have gone better.

Rev. Tim and Beth Heiney, **Guinea, West Africa**

People were really amazed with the work you did, as they could feel God's grace through your initiative. Some people from the government were also interested in the idea of the clinics and said that our town will always be open for you.

Rev. Alex Ziemann, **Brazil**

I've always thought MOST Ministries had a solid base Biblically. There must be a good missionary tradition behind MOST Ministries, because the model they have is excellent—first class. Respect, vision and very good organization.

Rev. Edmundo Rentana, **Costa Rica**

Appreciation from Team Members

I will never forget that trip to Haiti. What it did for me, inside my soul, was to call something out of me that I didn't think I was capable of doing or experiencing. It stretched me in many ways and I probably wouldn't be a pastor today had God not given me this opportunity to step out in faith and serve Him and the people in Haiti.

Rev. Lloyd Stuhr, team member **Haiti**

Over the past ten years as a team leader and board member, I am continuously amazed to watch God work through our team members by loving on those we serve and in return receiving so much love back. The field-driven focus of MOST has allowed me to watch ministries grow in many countries in all parts of the world.

Kevin Gambill, team leader, **Dominican Republic, Siberia, Guatemala, Mexico, Cambodia, Tanzania, Honduras, Brazil, Panama**

We were impressed by the organizational structure—the pre-field Servant Bible Study, the trained team leaders, the on-site logistics, and the back home re-entry process of MOST Ministries.

Rev. Don and Gerry Kirst, team members, **Uruguay, Latvia, India, China, Panama**

BEYOND SIGHT

God's Vision for Using Ordinary
People to Impact the World

Gayle Sommerfeld
with
Sandra Sommerfeld Helm

InspiringVoices®

Copyright © 2016 Gayle Sommerfeld with Sandra Helm.

All rights reserved. No part of this book may be used or reproduced by any means, graphic, electronic, or mechanical, including photocopying, recording, taping or by any information storage retrieval system without the written permission of the author except in the case of brief quotations embodied in critical articles and reviews.

Scriptures taken from the Holy Bible, New International Version®, NIV®. Copyright © 1973, 1978, 1984, 2011 by Biblica, Inc.™ Used by permission of Zondervan. All rights reserved worldwide. www.zondervan.com The "NIV" and "New International Version" are trademarks registered in the United States Patent and Trademark Office by Biblica, Inc.™ All rights reserved.

Cover design: Emily Kay Sunderland

Inspiring Voices books may be ordered through booksellers or by contacting:

Inspiring Voices
1663 Liberty Drive
Bloomington, IN 47403
www.inspiringvoices.com
1 (866) 697-5313
This book available as an ebook.

Because of the dynamic nature of the Internet, any web addresses or links contained in this book may have changed since publication and may no longer be valid. The views expressed in this work are solely those of the author and do not necessarily reflect the views of the publisher, and the publisher hereby disclaims any responsibility for them.

Softcover ISBN: 978-1-4624-1202-0
ebook ISBN: 978-1-4624-1203-7

Library of Congress Control Number: 2016915534

Print information available on the last page.

Inspiring Voices rev. date: 12/7/2016

Dedication

To Don, my much loved husband,

You were there from the beginning. Even though you never saw the captivating video, you caught the vision and joined me on the first team to Haiti, and decades later you are still here by my side sharing ministry experiences beyond our sight.

You were beside me, always encouraging me, as this book took on a life of its own. Digging up old records of past teams and ministry events was a review of all those years, giving us the opportunity to reflect and draw even closer to each other and to God.

Thank you.

Contents

Foreword

I first met Gayle Sommerfeld when I was a missionary in Panama serving as a volunteer coordinator. It was in 2002 that she arrived with a team of college students to serve several local ethnic groups. I could see from our first encounter that she was passionate about missions and very experienced at leading teams.

As a missionary I had hosted many mission teams from churches, schools and sending agencies, but the teams from Mission Opportunities Short Term (MOST Ministries) were in a class of their own. At that point in time I was unaware of the pre-field training Gayle required of her mission teams, but I saw the results in the teams that came to serve. They were culturally sensitive, had servant-student attitudes and her Team Leader model was one I had not encountered before. It made hosting teams easier and I was able to carry on with other work even when MOST Ministries' teams were in the field.

Gayle knew that God was working all over the world and that she was simply bringing teams to join Him in His work, considering it a privilege to serve His diverse people. I appreciated that approach to short-term missions so much that, years later, when I was working as a missionary in a different country, I contacted MOST Ministries about sending teams to that field. Even though coordinating mission teams and projects was not my particular area of work at that time, I saw needs and knew MOST Ministries could help, and they did.

That call to MOST Ministries strengthened our relationship and ultimately resulted in me working for the ministry several years later, first as a Team Administrator and then as the Executive Director. From inside the ministry I saw the preparation and details that resulted in the unique short-term teams I had experienced as a hosting missionary. The effort that goes into each mission team is extensive, but what I also saw as a staff member at MOST Ministries was Gayle's complete reliance on God and dedication to following His will.

I saw her live this out time and again in the office with projects, partnerships, staffing, and organizational issues. I once heard a co-worker describe Gayle's approach to problem solving as "you know she is on her knees," meaning she takes everything to the Lord in prayer. I have worked with Gayle for fourteen years and I know her *modus operandi* to be looking first and foremost to the Lord for direction and then moving forward in faith.

Beyond Sight is how Gayle has lived her life and is the legacy she has left for MOST Ministries. She gave the ministry a clear mission to effect change on earth *for Jesus Christ*, by mobilizing Christians in reaching those who do not yet know Christ, and doing it through short-term mission trips.

Carly Hatcher
Executive Director, 2007 – 2016
MOST Ministries

Acknowledgements

Our only daughter, Sandi, and I were having lunch in a diner in 2012. It was a routine that often occurred whenever I returned from a short-term mission trip. Sandi was doing her usual debriefing as I reflected on my experiences. The conversation took an unusual twist when Sandi suggested that it was time that I consider writing my memoirs on how Mission Opportunities Short Term (MOST Ministries) began. She encouraged me to document the history of the ministry for the sake of my grandchildren, in order to help them understand Don and me and our passion for spreading the love of Christ and caring for the many underserved people around the globe.

I said yes on the condition that she would assist me. That was four years ago and over those years we have come to see that God, in His infinite wisdom, had bigger plans for my writings than just a memoir for my grandchildren. The writing eventually grew into a manuscript with publishing guidelines and distribution potential well beyond our family. Just as MOST Ministries grew beyond our expectations, God was doing it again, growing the potential of our writing beyond what we expected!

When Sandi and I began this project, I was unaware of her passion and skill for writing. Early in the project when Sandi edited and even rewrote a portion of my writings, I was pleasantly surprised by the expertise with which she sorted through my many words and phrases, pulling out what was most important and then creatively expanding the piece with descriptions provided through our conversations. This became our pattern: I wrote, we talked and then Sandi rewrote.

As two untrained writers, we knew we needed outside help. God led us to Cindy Crosby, a substantive editor who helped us take the many unique team stories and organize them by geographical regions. Cindy also edited chapter content, helping to shape the book. Her knowledge and insight was immensely helpful.

Roxanne M. Smith and her husband, Andy, also offered wonderful insight. It was their editing that encouraged shorter chapters of my life, interspersed in the first section. Roxanne spent hours reviewing the book, chapter by chapter, despite a serious and painful back condition ·that restricted her ability to be upright for more than two hours a day. Roxanne's willingness to invest her precious time and energy into *Beyond Sight*, despite her own struggles, inspired and blessed us. Roxanne was also eager to help with practical writing advice, having written and published her own memoirs in *Struck Down, but Not Destroyed*.

Barb Collins was by our side from the very beginning as she carefully applied her editing skills through all the endless revisions. When we apologized for sending her yet another revision, she would cheerfully reply, "I am here to serve."

As the project grew our friends and family were there to help. Judy Rink faithfully invested in the creative process and encouraged us when we became weary. Several others read chapters, made suggestions, provided encouragement and remembered us in their prayers. Their enthusiastic response to the content kept us going. Thank you Jane Sharka, Kathy Blair, Dave Granner, Darrah Dickerson, Martha Roskam, the women of Sandi's Bible study group at Wheaton Bible Church, the members of our home church, Family In Faith, and the innumerable others who supported us.

Sandi's family was unwavering in their support, from beginning to end. They encouraged us while offering their own unique insights as they read revision after revision. Thank you Dave, Drew, Kate, Sarah and Becca!

As the writing progressed toward the final stages, draft copies were sent to our other children and their spouses for input: Scott and Cindy, Brad and Judy, and David and Jen. David had joined us on two of the early teams to Haiti. He was also a faithful editor during this writing process. Comments from family members in reviewing the draft were encouraging. Don and I are forever grateful for each one of them and their acceptance of our passion to serve the underserved.

God led us to gifted graphic artist, Emily Kay Sunderland, who in turn provided us with the exceptional book cover design! He also led us to Anne Camblin and Anie Salgado who joined the team at the last minute to make final edits.

My most faithful encourager has been Don who listened to endless pages of manuscript while I asked the same questions over and over again. "Is the point clearly stated? Does it reflect God's greatness?" I could not have completed this task without his untiring support and input. Don graciously made lunches for Sandi and me as we met and also volunteered to do other domestic chores, allowing me to focus on the writings. Thank you!

God has clearly been present during this incredible endeavor. He encouraged us through the support of others, inspired us through His Word and always reminded us to trust Him. It has been a privilege for us to work with so many to effectively tell the story of MOST Ministries and my many amazing ministry experiences. Those experiences reveal how God uses ordinary people to do the extraordinary. Thank you to all who helped with this project that allows us to show God's greatness in the past and inspires us to follow God's will for our future.

Part One

The Early Years

1

You Can Make a Difference

The wheels of the plane touched down, bouncing and skidding on the steaming hot tarmac. The view out the window revealed a very small airport surrounded by hundreds of tin huts. We were in Haiti! My husband Don and I looked at each other with excitement as we unfastened our seat belts and grabbed our bags from the overhead compartment. Our big adventure was about to begin.

We exited directly outside. The sun glared, and the air smelled of charcoal. We were greeted by a small band of musicians welcoming us with festive Haitian music. The cheerful, vacation-like atmosphere soon evaporated, however, as we made our way through customs, a crowded and noisy experience where we stood in long lines.

It didn't matter; I was thrilled to be standing there, energized by the new sights and sounds. Ever since feeling called by God more than a year ago, I had dreamt of this moment to serve Him on a short-term mission team in a foreign country.

It began with the video series, *You Can Make a Difference*, by Tony Campolo. It was the fall of 1987, and I was showing these videos to the teens in our youth group. I had hoped to help them see the plight of the poor around the world, but God had a special plan for Tony's message. He intended it for me.

His words reached into my soul and held me captive. It was as though Campolo's plea for viewers to consider going out into the world, making a difference in the name of Christ, was directed specifically to me. He spoke of the profound benefits of a short but meaningful visit to impoverished nations. My heart ached as the video showed clips of young Haitian children poorly clothed and visibly in need of food. I longed to go and help.

By the end, it was clear that God was asking me, *"Will you go into the world and make a difference in My name?"* After the youth left the room, I dropped to my knees in front of a folding chair, buried my head in my arms and passionately responded to God declaring, "Yes, Lord, I will go."

That afternoon I shared with Don how deeply I had been affected by Campolo's words. I told him about the commitment I had made to the Lord and wondered aloud, "How will God use me, a fifty-year-old wife, mother and grandmother?" But I trusted God. If He was calling me, He would use me. Don, who also has a heart for the poor, joined me in making a commitment to go wherever God called.

After the video and that intimate moment with God, I had expected a clear and obvious sign that God was calling us to go and serve, but nothing happened. When I explored the mission opportunities our church offered, I discovered they were only for long-term missionaries. I was inspired by the idea of going and serving for just a short time, but I was not sure how to do that on my own.

A year passed, and I continued to wait faithfully for a sign while I operated my in-home daycare business and continued to raise our youngest son, David, who was entering high school. Then Don and I attended a conference where we met Rev. Art Vincent, founder of Advancing Renewal Ministries (ARM), a non-denominational organization. He told us of his ministry, traveling to foreign countries with organized short-term mission teams and helping with construction work and other projects. We knew this was God's answer to our quest to serve Him on a foreign mission. Through this ministry, Don and I formed a team to travel to Haiti. Our mission: to finish construction on a new church.

That was just six months ago. Now it was March of 1989 and we were in Haiti! Our group of fourteen American team members stuck out in the crowd—obvious targets for beggars. The worst were the "porters." They would take a duffle bag, carry it a few feet, and then demand payment for their "assistance." The up thrust palm was the same in any language: "Pay up!" We had been warned that we were to clearly tell them, "No." With twenty-eight checked bags, many filled with clothing and quilts to donate, and our fourteen carry-ons, it was a challenging task to guard the luggage and keep it out of the hands of the aggressive porters.

With this in mind, Rev. Dale Arendt, our experienced team leader from ARM, instructed us to circle around the bags on the luggage carts. We awkwardly moved as one unit as we pushed the carts outside to connect with our Haitian host, Rev. Remus Arboret.

I was eager to meet this Haitian pastor; however, the chaos made introductions impossible. Dale and the pastor concentrated on the task at hand of escorting the people onto the bus and loading the luggage. It was amazing to watch the heavy bags being hauled to the top of the vehicle, securely strapped down, and covered with tarps, but we were even more amazed when we realized the pastor's helpers were settling in to travel the bumpy Haitian roads balanced on top of the mound of luggage!

As I took a seat on the bus, I looked around me. I couldn't help but stare. The streets were teeming with activity, slowing us down as we traveled through the capital city of Port-au-Prince. The *You Can Make a Difference* video and all my personal research had not prepared me for what my eyes, ears, and heart were experiencing.

There was a sea of people! They walked along the road, pedaled bikes, pushed carts, or led donkeys amid all the motorized traffic. The street activity consisted mostly of buses, trucks and motorcyclists. Haitians created mini roadside cafés as they cooked over charcoal fires.

Women, wearing brightly colored dresses, effortlessly carried baskets filled with fruits and baked goods on their heads. Men sat on delivery carts pulled by donkeys. Stray dogs roamed with their ribs clearly visible. The constant sound of honking vehicles filled the dusty air.

The buildings, usually one or two stories, were constructed from cement block. Many were covered with faded paint in red or blue, the national colors. Don and I were curious about all the uninhabitable half-built buildings that lined the streets. Why were so many buildings unfinished?

Glued to the window, I desperately tried to hold my camera still as the bus bounced over potholes while swerving to avoid the donkeys, *tap taps* (taxis) and bicyclists. As we traveled out of the city, the roads remained congested. The charcoal cook fires were replaced by bicycle repair services and small stands selling household items, like plastic buckets.

As I drank in the scenery, I thought of Haiti's sobering statistics as the poorest country in the Western Hemisphere with one of the highest infant and child mortality rates. It was hard to comprehend the struggles of the precious children I saw playing in the dirt. I prayed for their safety. Unfortunately for those who survived, there was little hope for education since there were no free government schools. As a result, the majority of Haitians were illiterate.

My heart ached. I wanted to do something that would change the facts and bring hope to the people. Working on the church, a place where people could go to learn about the love of Christ and the hope He brings, would be my way of making a small difference in this struggling nation.

Arriving at Rev. Arboret's home, we drove through a large metal gate into a courtyard. His home, like many others, was surrounded by a high-security wall made of cement block, topped with broken glass to prevent anyone from scaling the wall. The reverend's wife, Jamine, welcomed us warmly.

After we unloaded the bus, we gathered for a delicious meal of beans and rice, prepared by Jamine and her helpers. The room was filled with joyful commotion and conversation. I looked over at the youngest team member, an energetic teenage boy, to make sure he was adjusting well. He was laughing.

I remembered the day I first met many of these team members. Don and I had been asked to fill this newly forming Haiti team with people from our church. With excitement, I had eagerly contacted my peers, hoping to create a team of all our mission-minded friends, but that was not God's plan. I was disappointed when only two were able to commit.

Don and I had placed an announcement in the church bulletin. Discouraged that this team was not taking shape as I had envisioned, I had wanted to say to the strangers who were filling the room for our first meeting, "Who are you and who said you could go?" Instead, I managed to say, "Welcome, let's introduce ourselves and share why we are interested in going to Haiti."

Of course, after I heard their stories and what God was doing in their lives, I was humbled and grateful that they had responded. Over the course of the next few months, as we met to prepare, I had come to appreciate these multi-talented team members with diverse ages and personalities, perfectly chosen by God.

Since I helped organize the team, I felt a sense of responsibility for each member and was pleased that everyone seemed to be adjusting well. Thankfully, Rev. Arboret and Jamine spoke English, removing the language barrier. Over dinner, the pastor's love for his people and the Lord was evident as he shared about his ministry. As a young man he had traveled by foot and horseback throughout rural Haiti, sharing the love of Christ and planting churches. As a result, several hundred churches had been built. Many of his congregations began with just a few followers under a tree or a simple shelter. Over time he trained local pastors and these small gatherings developed into congregations, with simple cement block church buildings.

Our hosts explained that Haitians literally build their homes and churches brick by brick. They purchase each brick as they can afford it. Everything is paid for in cash; loans are uncommon for the average Haitian. Homes and churches can take months or years to complete, a slow process. The unfinished structures we saw in Port-au-Prince were either in the midst of building or, most likely, were abandoned. Often the owners could not afford to continue.

The poverty level in Haiti is staggering. Political oppression and corruption have plagued this island for centuries, preventing the economic growth of the populous. With few free schools, there is little opportunity for improvement.

We were disheartened to learn that due to the simple and rustic living conditions, the Haitians had been cutting trees for homes and firewood for generations without replanting. In many regions, the deforestation combined with heavy rains caused the erosion of the topsoil, leaving the current hard, barren surface. Farming was nearly impossible.

The Haitians struggle to survive. They do what they can to find food and create shelter. The pastor thanked us for coming, reminding us of the powerful impact it would have on his people, to see foreigners who cared enough to come and help. I hoped he was right.

I loved learning about this unique country, but eventually we said our goodnights and prepared for bed. Dropping my weary body onto the cot should have transported me into a deep sleep, but then I heard Protection and Strength, Rev. Arborets' two guard dogs. At the slightest movement outside, they sounded their canine alarms. I didn't know their names when I first heard their menacing bark, and at the time I would have named them something entirely different, like Persistent and Tireless.

The next morning our host explained that these dogs were there for our security and we should have been filled with confidence and peace when we heard them bark. When I met these ferocious-sounding canines I was surprised to see they were much smaller than their bark implied.

After breakfast, as our team boarded the bus for our next destination of Petit Goave, we were relieved to learn that Protection and Strength would not be accompanying us. Although thankful for the safety they had provided, we secretly hoped that our next accommodation's "security system" would be less noisy!

On our way to Petit Goave we made an unexpected stop in Cite Soleil, a suburb of Port au Prince. Rev. Remus needed to visit one of his churches recently damaged by Hurricane Gilbert. We were told that much of Cite Soleil had originally been built as temporary housing for 3,000 people in response to a large fire in Port au Prince. Decades later, it was now an impoverished permanent dwelling place for around 300,000 Haitians. Cite Soleil means "Sun City," a great name for a vacation spot, but this poverty stricken shantytown was far from desirable.

Due to the tight quarters we could not park our van near the church. We parked on the outskirts of the city and found ourselves walking down a narrow path. Walls of corrugated tin and cinder block, the only apparent building materials available, stretched as far as I could see. What felt like a maze of metal was really a path between tightly-packed tin huts. So narrow was the path at times that with arms stretched out on either side, I could almost touch opposite homes. Garbage was everywhere: plastic bags, bottles, and broken glass.

This city was not on the itinerary, yet while preparing for this trip, my eyes and heart had been drawn to the pictures of this community. I read articles describing the extreme poverty of Cite Soleil which created an unexplainable longing to see and meet the people living here. Now, as we ventured on foot down these winding metal corridors into the heart of the community, I felt like I was walking through those photographs. It was hard to believe I was really here.

I found it challenging to peer inside the huts. There were no windows to let the light in, just narrow openings for a doorway. I didn't want to be intrusive and stare, but quickly glanced inside one hut. There was only a single metal bed frame, which almost filled the small home.

The women cooked outside in the narrow walkway, using charcoal for fuel. I considered the daily struggles these families faced. How far would they have to walk to find clean water? I was overwhelmed. I had seen poverty before, but never like this. Don was also visibly moved by what he saw.

We were quite a sight for the Haitians. Fourteen "blancs," their word for a white man or woman, walking single file, stood out. Mothers pulled their children closer as they watched us with as much curiosity as we watched them. We offered smiles to put them at ease, but for many we were the first "blanc" they had ever seen.

As we approached the damaged church, we could see that several of the walls were lying in ruin. Drawing closer, I noticed, oddly enough, that there was a doorway with no walls—just an archway made from wire and a paper sign draped across the top reading, "Welcome to Boston 1," in English. I could only assume that this area of Cite Soleil was referred to as Boston 1. Standing there, taking in the sight of a doorway with no defining walls, I was impressed with the pride and dignity of the people who created this welcoming entrance amidst such destruction.

The church had one tin wall and one cement block wall. More than half of the roof was missing and what was left was propped up by two by fours. An altar and chair were placed under the propped up roof. Rubble was everywhere.

The local pastor welcomed us warmly—a faithful shepherd to his flock in spite of this severely damaged church.

After meeting local members of the congregation, we prepared to return to the bus. I took a moment to stop and take in my surroundings. I was beginning to understand my previous longing to see this city. God knew that I would have this opportunity to stand here. He placed in me the desire to see this mass of humanity, how they lived, and to have my heart broken. Although the visit was brief, the impact was deep.

As we continued on for several more hours of bumpy travel, I could not stop thinking about the people I had seen in Cite Soleil and the conditions in which they lived. Could I do anything to help these Haitians feel valued and to give them the hope found in Christ? Again, I thought of the church we were there to help build and prayed that it would bring encouragement to the people of southern Haiti.

We arrived in Petit Goave, where we were housed in Rev. Arboret's former orphanage. It was a comfortable, large, two-story building with running water. What a stark contrast to the tin homes we had just seen!

After settling in we gathered on the veranda overlooking the ocean. Listening to the gentle sound of the waves was relaxing. Closing my eyes I could imagine being at a resort on an exotic island. When I opened my eyes, however, there was garbage littering the beach, pigs rooting through the trash, and a wooden path on stilts that led to an outhouse over the water. Eyeing the outhouse, I was grateful that our accommodations provided indoor plumbing.

Returning to the veranda after dinner was a treat. In the absence of streetlights, the stars were dazzling against the dark sky. A majestic view of God's creation! It was serene and peaceful with the sound of the lapping water. As I allowed the calming ocean to relax me I prepared for sleep hoping that without the continuous barking of Strength and Protection I would sleep well.

Just as Don and I were settling in for the night, the streets erupted with loud shouts, drums, and shrill singing. We were informed "not to worry," it was the usual Saturday night voodoo street dance. They told us the dance was harmless and would end sometime during the night.

It was impossible to ignore, as I knew it was not harmless, but harmful to the soul of the voodoo worshiper. I remembered reading that the majority of Haitians practiced voodoo, the worship of evil spirits. Praying for peace for myself and for the ritual dancers, I focused on trying to sleep.

We were informed "not to worry," it was the usual Saturday night voodoo street dance.

The night air was hot, heavy and filled with mosquitoes that took great pleasure in buzzing around my ears. As I alternated between covering my head to stop their annoying noise, and uncovering due to overheating, I resigned myself to another sleepless night. Remembering St. Paul's encouragement to "praise God in all circumstances" (1 Thessalonians 5:18), I tried hard to focus my thoughts on God and not on my misery.

Somehow the night passed, and morning dawned, bringing with it its own new sounds. Lying in bed I wondered to myself, *where did the donkeys come from and why must they have a conversation with the roosters so early in the morning?*

We began our day with great anticipation for the church service we would attend with Rev. Arboret. Looking over the veranda of our guesthouse, I noticed that the courtyard below was filling up with pastors from his distant churches. Many, having walked for hours to attend this special service, arrived carrying their best suits, shirts and ties in plastic bags over their shoulders. Others, having arrived earlier, were settled in the courtyard listening to Rev. Arboret's teachings. As they worshiped, they frequently broke into song. I loved the sound of the deep male Haitian voices, singing in unison. It sounded like a heavenly choir, especially in contrast to the noise of the previous night's voodoo worshipers.

We had been told that it was a 10:00 o'clock service. It was now after 10:00 and we feared we were late. Our American desire was to be punctual, but we were at the mercy of our Haitian host to transport us. At 11:00 a.m. our bus finally arrived; it was a lesson in the Haitians' more relaxed view towards timing.

We were led to the front of a very large church and seated on a raised platform overlooking a sea of faces. There were almost a thousand people present! Hundreds of colorful construction paper flags hung from the ceiling. The women were standing, singing, swaying and waving white handkerchiefs. Again I thought I was listening to a choir from heaven.

In Haiti, no woman would be in church without a hat, and that included us. We were prepared. For church we were told we were to wear hats and skirts or dresses. What we didn't know was the extent of attention that Haitian women paid to their Sunday morning attire and the beautiful dresses they owned. We were told later that these fine dresses were the castoffs sent from America and sold on the streets for pennies.

I found it embarrassing to be seated on the stage in my casual resale shop dress. Not wanting to look like rich North Americans, everyone had decided to dress simply. We came prepared to do construction work in our skirts and that is what we wore to church. Our Haitian sisters, however, came for worship in their finest clothes.

Rev. Dale Arendt was the guest pastor that day. He exhorted the congregation to give up their practice of relying on voodoo fetishes and charms for protection. He knew the Haitian culture was deeply rooted in the worship of demons, practiced out of fear of what these evil spirits would do if homage was not paid to them.

Rev. Arendt shared how God sent His son as His sacrificial offering for us, paying the debt of our sins and freeing us from a life of fear. The one true God, not the gods of their voodoo practices, is all powerful and yet only asks for our

...give up their practice of relying on voodoo fetishes and charms for protection.

faithful love—no need to sacrifice chickens, wear charms or perform dances, he said.

We had been asked to share our testimony. Several members spoke of their personal walk with the Lord, telling how a loving God transformed their lives. My heart yearned for all Haitians to hear the message of the life changing effects of knowing Christ. Seeing the ministry of Rev. Remus Arboret and the Haitians who were enthusiastically worshipping in this church gave me hope that the Word of God was spreading throughout this nation.

As the service was coming to an end, Rev. Arboret invited all the pastors, about 100 of them, to come forward and shake our hands as we asked God to bless their ministries. It was a humbling experience, as I thought about the many miles some of them had walked, just to worship with us. It was my honor to be in their presence. As I took each pastor's hand, I offered up a prayer for strength and wisdom as they tried to break through the strong voodoo beliefs of their communities.

Rev. Arboret invited members of the congregation to come forward for prayer with the team members. Thankfully, he had explained earlier that this might happen, since praying for healing was a common request. We were advised to hold the person's hands and ask a blessing as the Lord led us. We prayed for God's grace and that He would guide us in how to pray. About 200 Haitians responded to the prayer invitation.

The service came to an end. When we realized how close we were to our lodging, we chose to walk back, eagerly talking among ourselves. This was not a typical Sunday morning worship experience and we needed some time to process the blessings we had experienced.

After lunch we set out on foot for a personal mission of mine: to find a school Don and I had read about in a devotional booklet lent to us by Don's coworker. This devotional referred to an American man, Harry Brakeman, and his connections to many schools in this city. Since the government did not provide free education for the children, most schools were funded by private sources. Many charged fees that poor families could not afford.

Thankfully, Mr. Brakeman's schools were able to provide an education for each child enrolled for only ten American dollars per year. That covered the child's tuition, uniform, and a daily meal. Before the trip I had enthusiastically informed my friends about the schools, collecting $240 dollars to be donated. It was my hope and prayer that we would be able to personally deliver this money.

We knew the name of the founder, but did not know exactly where to find him. Sharon, an American nurse living in Haiti who spoke Creole, was traveling with us. She thought she could find him. We all set out on foot. Getting there turned out to be a bit of an adventure, especially since we did not have exact directions. There were no street signs or other markers. We would stop, and a Haitian would tell us to look for this landmark, or that landmark.

Eventually, over an hour later, we found a very astonished Harry Brakeman. We explained who we were and that we had collected money to donate to his schools. He thanked us and was extremely grateful. He explained that earlier that day a Haitian pastor, working with one of the schools in the mountains, had come to him saying that he had 200 students and no money for their daily meals.

My God...could orchestrate a plan to answer this pastor's prayer, miles away and months before...

It was an honor to hand Mr. Brakeman the money, realizing that it was part of God's special plan to care for these 200 Haitian children. I should not have been surprised that my God, the creator of the universe, could orchestrate a plan to answer this pastor's prayer, miles away and months before it was even uttered, but I was.

It was exciting to sense that we were exactly where God wanted us to be. He was using us to answer the prayers of others. I prayed that God would continue to lead our team and was eager to see what God had in store for us in the coming week.

As the day came to an end and I reflected on God's amazing plan to care for the school children, my thoughts drifted to one of my own childhood memories—an unfortunate situation where I had been told I was "less than" and unworthy, due to family circumstances beyond my control. I thought of the children in Haiti, in circumstances beyond their control. How did they feel? Did they know they are valued in God's eyes? I prayed that the pastor running the school was encouraging the children by sharing God's love, just as my mother had shared with me.

As I lay down to sleep, I heard again the hurtful words of my friend and considered the many events of those early years.

2

Through the Eyes of a Child

"I can't play with you anymore," my friend declared.

"Why not?" I asked, surprised and confused.

"Because you don't have a father."

When I was four years old, I always went to my friend's kitchen window and knocked, our signal for her to come out and play. This time, instead of running outside, she talked to me through the open window.

Not understanding, I replied, "I do *too* have a father!" Although he lived far away and I had only met him a few times, I knew he existed. I tried to convince her, but my friend didn't budge.

Crushed and confused I ran home to tell my mother. She was not surprised. She knew better than I the implications of a home without a father in the early 1940's.

When I was born in the spring of 1937, my family was in a state of turmoil. My father left my mother, brother, sister and me and moved to Chicago. We remained in Holland, Michigan. My parents didn't divorce, but they lived separately, with separate lives.

This created a scandal. My family no longer fit the norm of what was expected of a traditional home in our conservative town. My mother was a strong and resourceful woman. She worked hard at a local factory to support us and rarely complained. Thankfully, with her eight siblings close by, there were many extended family members to help.

Before this unfortunate event with my friend, I was unaware of the stigma of our situation. I felt safe and secure in my family. I was the youngest child. Hazel, my sister, was the oldest at nine years my senior, and Gordon, my brother, was seven years my senior. Until the incident with my friend, I felt loved and content. For the first time, I felt the sting of rejection.

A neighboring widow had compassion on me. She often invited me into her home to look at books together and pass the time. Through her kindness my world began to feel safe again. The widow's actions were simple, yet profound for me, a lonely little girl. It wasn't long before I entered kindergarten and no one mentioned anything about my father.

At the end of my kindergarten year my mother told us we would be moving to Chicago to live with my father. I remember the excitement of packing up my dolls and teddy bear for this grand adventure. I had never visited my father in Chicago and did not know where it was. Although the move was exciting, it was also difficult saying goodbye to my cousins and my home with several bedrooms and a big backyard.

My excitement soon turned to confusion as I learned that my new home was a tiny second floor apartment located above a bakery and meat market. My disappointment grew as I realized there was only ·one bedroom for all five of us. My outdoor play space was a small concrete slab, separated from an alleyway by an old broken wooden fence. I wondered, *where will I sleep? Where will I play?* I was told that it was temporary but this tiny apartment became my permanent home. Eventually things were sorted out and I adjusted to sleeping on the couch in the living room. My brother and sister slept in the dining room on daybeds. My mother was very creative in making our new home functional.

During this transition family routines, like gathering for dinners, were especially comforting. The kitchen was small, barely big enough for a family of five. With my father working two jobs, he was seldom home. As we gathered for dinner my mother always said a blessing over the food before we ate. Afterwards we were not excused from the table until the "Family Altar" devotions were read. We learned to give thanks and praise to God, and this encouraged me.

A close bond developed in the kitchen between my mother and I as we washed the dishes. My mother loved hymns. One of her favorites was "I Come to the Garden Alone." Her clear voice would fill the tiny kitchen as we laughed and sang. It was during these times that I could feel her warmth and love, helping me adjust to my changing world. I would often join in the chorus:

"And he walks with me, and He talks with me,
And He tells me I am His own;
And the joy we share as we tarry there,
None other has ever known."

My mother believed these words with all her heart. She knew the joy of Christ. He had helped her through many difficult circumstances and she continued to lean on Him.

One of the most wonderful gifts that my mother gave me was the knowledge that God was not just for Sunday mornings. He was to be thanked and praised throughout every day. I found great solace in ending my days with my mother kneeling beside me, talking to God.

My excitement over living with my father soon waned. He was a quiet, stern man who seldom showed any affection. No hugs or encouraging words. He worked long hours as a bus and taxi driver. When he was home he was tired, bringing tension into our tiny little apartment.

One day he told my sister to help my mother with the dishes. She said, "I'm busy." Then he told my brother to help my mother and he said, "I'm busy." I remember thinking; *I will try that, too.* However, when I said, "I'm busy." I got an angry shove from my father. It sent me flying through the room. I crashed over the windowsill, knocking the screen out. In slow motion I saw the cement from the alley below come up to meet me. I was terrified!

Somehow, before I fell completely out of the window, someone caught hold of me and dragged me back in. I could not stop crying. It left me gasping for breath for what seemed like hours.

My mother must have had a talk with my father. She came to me as I was cowering in the bedroom and promised that if he ever hit me again she would pack us up and take a train back to Michigan. I knew

I could trust her, but I remained fearful of my father. He never shoved or pushed me again, but our relationship was scarred.

I did my best to adjust to city life, but at a young age I felt a strong desire to leave. I planned to move out after high school, but this was against the norm. A woman did not typically leave her parents' home until she married.

When my sister graduated, she landed a good job in downtown Chicago as a secretary and was content to remain at home. My brother spent time in the military, only to return home as he enrolled in local university courses. I could not imagine remaining in that tiny tension-filled apartment one moment longer than necessary.

My desire to leave was so strong that in fifth grade I wrote a letter to a local university asking, "How do I get into college?" They responded with a required high school class list and suggested I make good grades. I felt excited. I was already an excellent student who loved to learn. When I read the response, I knew that my new goal in life was to go away to college.

I also had another dream: to work on a ship carrying freight to foreign lands, allowing me to see and experience new cultures, but I knew that, as a girl, my future was limited. My only option to leave home was to go to college. Maybe it would provide opportunities for me to see new sights.

While in the eighth grade, we took a road trip to Florida. I was thrilled, but I was unprepared for the open racial discrimination that was taking place in the South. It was a surprise, as we stopped at many restaurants, that there was a "Colored Restroom" and a regular "Restroom". In my northern naivety I always wanted to go into the Colored Restroom to see what color it was. My family told me to "hush up." Reluctantly, I went to the plain old white tile restroom, envying those who could go into the colored one.

I was upset when I finally understood what those signs meant. It was difficult to believe that African Americans were viewed as so inferior that we could not even share a common restroom! Sadly, I realized I had not seen many African Americans at the tourist stops along the way. I wondered just how restricted their lives were.

Although I enjoyed the adventure of traveling to the southern states, my new understanding of segregation bothered me. Just as I knew my childhood friend had been wrong in her judgment of my family, I knew that this was also wrong. I wished I could do something, like my kind neighboring widow, to try to heal the wounds of those who felt "less than."

3

Haiti, a Land of Grace

Once again I was awakened by the unique sounds of Haitian roosters and donkeys. It was day three of our 1989 Haiti construction team. We gathered for breakfast, ready to travel south and finally begin our assigned construction task. We soon learned that God had different plans.

"Our roofing materials did not arrive for the church in the south," announced Rev. Arboret during our breakfast in his former orphanage in Petit Goave. "So we will be redirecting this team to work on the damaged church in Cite Soleil."

I was ecstatic at the opportunity to spend more time in that community, but also humbled and awed as I realized that God had drawn me to the articles, preparing my heart for this change of plans. Fortunately, Rev. Arboret was able to order and guarantee the arrival of the construction materials needed for this new worksite.

When we arrived, the cement blocks had been delivered and stacked in an open area, about 100 feet from the church. Our first task was to carry them, one at a time, down the narrow path to the church.

Our North American way of thinking told us to remove and discard the broken cement blocks and splintered wood currently scattered across the church floor, providing a place to stack the new cement blocks. As we organized the team to remove the rubble, we were quickly informed that we should not discard what we thought of as trash because the pastor thought of it as his treasure. The pastor had a plan. He knew that the broken pieces could be used to build up the current floor of the church that was routinely covered with two to three inches of water during the rainy seasons. He knew how important it would be for the church to offer a dry refuge for the people.

...we should not discard what we thought of as trash because the pastor thought of it as his treasure.

We then learned he had been sleeping there every night for six months to protect these treasures from thieves. I was humbled by his sacrificial act. The blinders fell from my eyes and I looked around with new understanding of the hallowed ground on which we were standing. We carefully collected these treasures and found a corner in which to stack them.

The new blocks were carried, one at a time, with everyone assisting. The Haitian women gracefully walked down the path, each balancing a block on their heads. I tried and failed miserably!

As we worked, I was aware of one beautiful young woman wearing what seemed like a spotless white dress, making many trips balancing the blocks. She had such a presence about her that she seemed to glow. We had only a brief moment to talk. Through an interpreter, I learned that her name was Roxanne and that she described herself as "single for the Lord." Roxanne never intended to marry; she considered herself married to Jesus. I thought of her as a deaconess, or a nun. I hoped that I would have another opportunity to speak with her.

With the blocks secured at the church we could now bring in the bags of cement with a wheelbarrow. The challenge was how to mix the cement in that small area under the propped up roof. The blazing sun made it impossible for anyone to work out in the open. In the end, there were a dozen hot, sweaty people crowded into that small shady space trying to stay out of the way of the two people mixing the cement. Too many people, and far too hot!

While working at the church we met the pastor's son, Immanuel. He was studying English and speaking with him was a delight. He also had three friends—Garfield, Avril and Augustine—who came to us to practice their English. They were around twenty years old and were taking formal English classes there in Cite Soleil. Several of us followed these young men to meet their North American English teacher, a welcome break from the crowded work site. They led us through the narrow passageways. I loved exploring beyond the church, seeing the people and experiencing the culture.

After meeting their teacher, they also introduced us to more Americans: Diane, a nurse who ran a much-needed infirmary that she opened two hours a day, and another woman who was hoping to help the local Haitians by selling their artwork back in the United States.

The dedication of the teacher, nurse, and business entrepreneur encouraged me. Each one committed to serving the people of Boston 1, Cite Soleil. These four young men helped me to see a bigger and brighter picture. It was evident God was working in this place, giving these young men hope in the midst of their environment.

I was also encouraged as I thought about Don, who had stayed back at the house to meet with Rev. Arboret, discussing future ministry projects. Don, a successful grant writer, was inspired to use his skills to help the reverend fund projects that would benefit the community. They explored ideas such as purchasing a large fishing boat to support a fishing cooperative, allowing local fishermen to fish in deeper waters.

Back at the church the local community was alive with curiosity. We were like a reality TV program right at their front door. For many this was their first experience of seeing white people from the United States.

A Haitian mother approached a female team member and held out her child. The team member took the child and spoke adoringly to it. After a few moments an interpreter approached and stated, "The woman is asking you to take her child, keep it and bring it back with you to the United States. I think you had better give the child back." She did. Haitian mothers continued to ask members to hold their children, believing that the touch of a white woman with blonde hair would bring their child good luck.

They were desperate for a better life. Earlier, a young boy approached Don stating, "I will be your son. You can be my father. I will work for you. You can bring me back to the United States and I will stay with you." It was difficult to say no.

23

Children gathered around us at the site. Little girls wore oversized t-shirts while the little boys frequently wore no clothing at all. I was told that the Haitians often do not dress their little boys because they are so proud of having sons. Their little naked bodies testified to their masculinity.

It was obvious that many Haitians viewed girls and women as "less than." We learned that a young girl, who was watching us and very noticeably in her ninth month of pregnancy, was only fifteen years old. Sadly, she had been used by her father as a source of income. He made her "services" available for a fee.

It was hard to see such suffering and abuse of the young women of Cite Soleil. Wanting to rescue them all I cried out to God, *"Where is Your justice? Surely You care deeply for these children."* It was hard to watch and not jump in, trying to be a savior to all. I

I cried out to God, "Where is Your justice … for these children?"

wanted a quick fix. I didn't have any patience for this kind of suffering. My only hope was that through Christ, lives could be changed and this church would be an instrument of that change.

With the audience of children and adults that came to observe our work, we were grateful that we were making progress. The walls were higher and one was completed. As we were admiring it, one of the team members casually leaned on the wall. The cement wasn't hardened between the blocks! The wall came tumbling down. Fortunately, no one was hurt.

But now we knew the difference between trash and treasure. We added this rubble to the treasure pile, knowing it would be put to good use. Then, we diligently began building a new wall.

"Chante, chante" I called out, standing alone in the midst of the maze of tin walls. It was the second day of working at the Cite Soleil church. I had wandered just a little from the worksite when I heard what sounded like women singing in the distance. Intrigued, I tried to locate where the sound was coming from, but with no success.

Desperate to find what I hoped was a gathering of Haitian women, I had resorted to standing in the middle of the path, and calling out the only Creole word I knew for singing, "chante." What a sight I must have been, a "blanc" making a racket in broken Creole.

Finally, someone understood my plea and led me to the source. There, in a crowded hut filled with women from the church and sitting on the cardboard covered floor, was Roxanne, Bible in hand, leading the women in Bible study. I felt like an explorer who had found the day's treasure.

I hurried back to the work site to find someone who could interpret for me. I returned with Garfield, who attempted to help me explain to the women that I had come from the United States with kits to make small banners.

In preparation for the trip my Bible study group had helped me assemble twenty kits. I had hoped to connect with the Haitian women. The banners were brightly colored, with the words "joy," "hope," and "peace." Garfield tried to help me explain that if they would return tomorrow, we could make the banners together. The women shook their heads no. They said, "We will be busy."

Then they began to inquire, "What is a banner?" As I explained it to Garfield, he suddenly understood and translated the word banner into "flag."

What a change! They were enthusiastic and committed to return. I could hardly believe my good fortune. God was continuing to give me the desires of my heart; I was in Cite Soleil and would soon be enjoying the company of these Haitian women.

Those twenty flag kits were just enough. With the assistance of two other team members, as well as Garfield and Immanuel as translators, we explained the messages of joy, hope and peace, and how they come from Jesus. We also explained how to use the needle and thread when stitching the letters to the banner. The skill level of the women varied. Some were obviously experienced, while others needed more assistance.

The home in which we gathered was typical for this area, about eight-by-eight foot square, with a dirt floor covered with cardboard. The only furniture was a bed. The women did not mind. They sat on the cardboard-covered flooring, the bed or stood. Several were outside. There was a lot of laughter as we worked together on the flags that would brighten their simple homes.

The cardboard was placed on the floor of the home with the same purpose as a rug in America. When it rained, the cardboard was stored somewhere off the ground. We were told that when this area floods, water can stand in the houses for weeks. With one bed and six to eight people in the home, the Haitians took turns sleeping. Someone used the single metal-framed bed throughout the day and night.

Roxanne was certainly a spiritual mentor for these women and became an inspiration for me. She was always dressed in a sparkling white dress, ironed crisp, which she used as her "habit" as though she were a nun. After all, she did say she was single for Jesus.

One afternoon, through the help of an interpreter, she invited me to go to her home. There were no additional interpreters available to go with us, and we were supposed to stay close to the work site. I trusted her to take good care of me. I also wanted to be fully immersed in the community and not part of a group activity of "blancs" on tour. I was grateful for the personal invitation.

It seemed like we walked a long way. I began to question my judgment to go alone. Being the only "blanc" in that slum seemed threatening, and I was having trouble keeping up with Roxanne. As we walked, there was a dead dog in the path. The sunlight was shining on all the fleas that were hopping on and off the carcass. I took a big step over the dog and continued along.

Then there was a group of young men talking in the middle of the path. They took no notice of me trying to pass by them. Roxanne was ahead of me and I needed to catch up with her. These boys were standing close to the edge of a ditch that was filled with a sea of garbage. It looked like a cauldron alive with everything evil.

Cautiously I stepped around the young men, putting myself on the brink of the ditch. Terrified, I realized that all any one of those boys had to do was to shift their weight my way and I would have toppled over the edge, but they left me alone.

Relieved to finally catch up with Roxanne, I stayed close as she led me to the home that she shared with her sister's family, a husband and their two children. There was a bare bulb hanging from the ceiling and I noticed the electric iron Roxanne used to press her "habit." As she introduced me to her sister, I regretted that I did not have an interpreter. I did my best with hand gestures and smiles yet longed for the ability to go beyond such limited interaction.

My visit was short. Soon we were heading back to the work site. With less congestion and walking a little slower, I was able to stop and snap a picture of the large garbage filled ditch.

Unfortunately, going to Roxanne's home did have some lasting consequences. When I returned to the church I was aware of a radiating heat under my skirt. My legs were on fire! It was painful and hard to endure. I didn't know what it was until we returned to Remus' home. There was the evidence. The fleas from the dead dog were looking for a warm body and they found it—mine. I had bites from my midriff to my ankles. Thankfully, those hundreds of fleabites did not result in serious complications, but I became a walking advertisement for calamine lotion, pink from the chest down. Ultimately, there was not much sleep to be had that night either.

In contrast to the living conditions we witnessed, we were all aware of the high level of personal cleanliness of the people. They often bathed in what little bit of water they had. Their homes were sparse, but neat. The pastor's wife dusted the church altar and chair several times a day. She kept things orderly even though it appeared to us to be hopeless with all the dust and debris. We marveled at her, and wondered if we would put forth the effort to be as clean and neat if we were in her circumstances. I began to see her as a silent witness, as she showed her reverence for God's house.

... a silent witness, as she showed her reverence for God's house.

There was one thing left in my grab-bag of "cross cultural things to do" while I was in Haiti. It was our last day at the work site, and I was hoping to tell the children a flannelgraph story I had prepared. Each day I had come prepared with my small portable felt board and story felt figures, but there had never been an interpreter available to make it happen.

I had presented this story many times for Sunday school classes, and had the message memorized. All I needed was an audience of children and an interpreter. Finally, it happened. We gathered in one corner outside the church with my flannelgraph board. I simply asked the interpreter to hold the board as I placed the figures on it.

It was challenging to speak through an interpreter. When I told flannelgraph stories at home, I loved watching the faces of the children as the stories unfolded. It inspired me! As these children crowded closer to the board, they turned their backs to me. They were looking at the figures and listening intently to the interpreter. They loved the story, however I might as well have been a non-participating bystander. There was no encouraging eye contact or facial expressions to indicate if they understood. All I could see was the backs of their heads as I reached over them to add new figures.

I questioned my motives. Could I step aside and let the message and the interpreter be the focus? The fact that I felt so let down was my answer. I needed to adjust my focus away from me and onto Christ, knowing it was the message that was important—not the messenger.

With all these activities—making banners with the women, visiting Roxanne's family, and storytelling with the children, I was able to stay out of the way of the team members who were mixing cement and laying blocks. While they were building the physical structure, several of my team members and I were attempting to build relationships despite the language barrier.

> *... it was the message that was important—not the messenger.*

I was grateful for those who were able to faithfully work in the hot sun, building the walls. Each day, after the team left in the late afternoon, the Haitian workers continued setting the re-rods for support and laying the blocks. With all the hard work we believed that the walls would soon be standing firm.

On our last day, as I prepared emotionally to say goodbye to this community, I looked at the huts surrounding the church and wondered about the health of the families living here. Did they have access to medical help? Were there doctors that they could turn to when illness struck? What about medications? I was concerned, having seen signs of illness and injuries having gone untreated. As I considered their dire situation, I felt God was calling me to return with doctors and nurses, in an attempt to bring hope and healing to these often forgotten people. I was encouraged by the thought of returning. I did not want this to be a final goodbye.

Our time in Haiti drew to a close. I had mixed emotions about leaving. It helped that we could participate in the dedication of the church building before we left.

When we arrived at the dedication, we entered through a proper doorway, the floor had been swept and the rubble neatly stacked. A few benches were brought in for our team and the Haitian helpers. The roof still needed to be replaced and the floor repaired, but the four walls were standing firm.

There was a brief ceremony and the presentation of a large banner that our team had made as part of our preparations. We expected it to be used in a rural church in southern Haiti, but God knew its destination would be this church in overpopulated, impoverished Cite Soleil. The banner was perfect with the word 'Allelu' emblazoned across the top with the brilliant golden sun underneath and five colorful figures with arms outstretched in praise.

After the brief dedication ceremony on site, we went to another church in the area to continue the celebration. That church could accommodate the whole team and the members of Boston 1. Many unique musical instruments were passed around and we were encouraged to join in playing with the Haitian ensemble. Such joy filled the room as we all came together in praise and worship.

Don had come prepared to talk at this gathering. He gave a testimony with such emotion that he had difficulty speaking. I was also feeling emotional, surprised at how deeply I felt connected to this land and these individuals. When Tony Campolo spoke in his video about the positive impact of going and serving people around the world, I had not anticipated the powerful effect this act would have on me. Experiencing the genuine friendship and love offered to us by the welcoming Haitian hosts, while sharing moments of worship, was life changing.

It was our last breakfast and an opportunity to thank Rev. Arboret and Jamine for their hospitality. They had provided so well for all our physical needs: a safe place to sleep and delicious meals. They had also offered us love and friendship.

The previous night, in an effort to share with others the impact this experience was having on my soul, I was inspired to write a poem. Now, after breakfast, I stood and shared with all, through this written work, how God had used this trip to open my heart to the people of Haiti.

An Ode to Cite Soleil

I opened my eyes and I wanted to shout
"Look Lord" there is garbage all about.

And people too, among the heaps of trash,
And lots of charcoal fires filling the air with ash.

And traffic and horns and squealing brakes
"Be careful, watch out!" for Heaven's sake!

Going up and down narrow mountain road beds
Haitians walking everywhere with pails upon their heads.

They all look alike Lord – so many the same
How could I ever remember their funny sounding names?

There is Remus, Jamine, Francois, Arnel and all the others.
Somehow they make me feel like we are all sisters and brothers.

Then we see the Cite Soleil, so crowded, so poor.
And a church with no walls, but look, it has a door.

No Lord, this church is hopeless, it can't be done.
But then we meet the people, one by one.

Avril, Augustine, Garfield, and Immanuel the Pastor's son.
They are so bright and eager and wanting to make fun.

They sang and prayed and teased everyone.
You'd think that living in Cite Soleil was quite a lot of fun.

How can that be, Lord, in the midst of poverty and disease.
Answer my question, Lord, tell me please.

Are these Your people, Lord, who like Job in distress
Did not curse You even though his life was a mess.

He spoke of praises to You and showed You respect.
Even though he must have felt like an insignificant speck.

You blessed Job, Lord, for trusting in You.
Brother Remus has shown us that he can trust You, too.

With his many churches—some faithful—some not
Guide him and bless him, he needs You a lot.

And for Jamine who stands tall by his side
Bless her Lord and always in her abide.

She has a quiet spirit and a servant's heart
Let us not forget her now that we are apart.

The answer, Lord? Now it's all so clear;
I was so deaf, but now I can hear.

Haiti is not a Land of Poverty, but a Land of GRACE!
Thank You, Lord, for bringing me to this wonderful place.

The poem helped me to bring closure to this amazing journey. When I arrived, my bags were packed with clothes and quilts to give away. Now I was leaving with a few Haitian souvenirs and a heart overflowing with treasures of the Spirit, the best souvenirs of all. This nation and its people impacted me deeply and I definitely was not the same person who had arrived only seven days earlier.

Our team had accomplished the given task; the church was near completion, but God, in His infinite wisdom, had so much more in mind for me than the rebuilding of that physical church. I felt as though He was beginning a process of rebuilding me from the inside out. I had experienced new joys as well as sorrows; my world was bigger and yet smaller. I saw God at work everywhere and I was humbled to have joined Him in His work in Haiti. I was ready to return home, but felt that maybe I would return someday. Was God encouraging me to respond to the medical needs I saw? Would I be able to meet such a challenge as providing medical care for Haitians?

During our flight home, I reached over and took Don's hand. I was thankful for his tender heart for the Haitians. I knew that together we could tackle whatever challenges God placed before us. As I leaned back in my seat I closed my eyes and remembered my youthful journey that eventually led me to this man.

4

Fire Eater to Fiancé

"Why do you need to go to college? Why can't you work like your sister, as a secretary?"

The tensions between my father and I continued throughout my high school years. He repeatedly told me that I should find a job after graduation, like my sister, and forget about college. Like many in his generation, my father had ended his schooling after the fourth grade to help his family. He did not see why a woman would want to continue beyond the twelfth grade.

With an adventurous spirit and a love of learning I knew that times were changing and I could aspire to new careers for women. My father did not understand. He refused to sign for my scholarships. With my mother's permission, I signed for him.

When my high school graduation day arrived, I was not surprised when all of my family members said they were too busy to attend the ceremony. They had never attended any of my school activities. I made one last plea on my graduation day. "I will be sitting on the stage, singing with a quartet, and receiving a scholarship!" I told them. I was all dressed up when I left, alone and discouraged, to catch a bus for my big night.

After arriving, I put on my graduation attire and entered the stage with my classmates who were also being honored. Then, halfway through the ceremony, I saw them. I watched in astonishment as my whole family entered and took their seats in the back row of the balcony.

When my brother saw me on stage, he left the auditorium to go to the store across the street. He bought a camera and came back in time to take pictures of me receiving my diploma.

To my amazement my father was openly proud. He said loudly as he greeted me after the ceremony, "There she is, the one who sat on the stage, the one who received a scholarship!" What a change! We even went to a restaurant for dinner. It's my only memory of our family going out to a restaurant for a celebration. It felt good.

Before I knew it, I was packing my bags and heading to college. Thinking I would enjoy a smaller school, I chose a Christian college near my Michigan relatives. Unfortunately, during the first year, it became evident that this college was not the right fit for me. This school held firmly to some very strict rules with which I did not agree. Going to the movies was forbidden and I had a stern housemother. This was not the college experience I had expected.

I transferred to a larger state school, the University of Illinois, for my sophomore year. I settled quickly into dorm life. With no strict housemother looking over my shoulder, I felt free to be myself.

My roommate was a perfect fit. She was a Christian, attending the Lutheran chapel. Although I had grown up in a different denomination, I decided to join her. Over time this chapel became my spiritual home, providing me with strong Christian friends.

My social life revolved around the college group at the chapel and the men in the Lutheran fraternity, Beta Sigma Psi. I enjoyed the intellectual challenges of my classes, and my weekends were filled with friends and social events.

One night at a fraternity party, one of the guys began juggling tennis balls. Next, he did a fire-eating routine! I found out later he had learned it when he worked at the state fair. I was not impressed; it seemed too dangerous.

I was impressed, however, when it came to academics. It turned out that this fire-eater, Donald Sommerfeld, was in my Earth Sciences class of two hundred and fifty students and getting some of the highest test scores. It didn't take me long to figure out who I wanted to sit near. I began looking for Don and asked him to help me study. He agreed and we began a nice routine. Don was kind and respectful. As we visited, we found we had similar interests, like travel and art.

It was not long before we began dating, but my goals were still firm. I was in college to get an education and was not pursuing a long-term relationship. So when Don nervously asked me to marry him, just six months after we met, it came as a complete surprise!

He also asked me about my relationship with God. I stumbled through a response, assuring him of my faith, and told him gently that I wasn't ready to give him an answer about marriage. Don agreed that I should spend some time thinking and praying before giving him a definite answer.

Later that night, I returned to my room. I thought about how marriage could change my life. I wondered—*if I married Don, would I stay focused on my schooling?* Don and I had such a wonderful connection and I always looked forward to the time we spent together.

Not sure what to do, I knelt before my bed and began praying, asking God for direction. What happened next is hard to explain, other than to say I heard an audible voice, God's voice, saying very clearly *"Marry Don Sommerfeld."* My heart raced as I asked again for God's direction and again it was as though I heard God telling me *"Marry Don Sommerfeld."* Whether the voice was truly audible or simply so strong in my soul that it echoed in my mind, I will never know, but it was clear to me that God had answered my prayers in a way that I had never experienced before. Don the "fire eater" soon became Don my fiancé.

5

Faith, Trust and Perseverance

Oh Lord, where do you want me? I wrote in my journal. I sat on my couch, overwhelmed by the incredible comforts of my home. The seven days spent in Haiti left me yearning to return. Instead of fading as time passed, the desire grew stronger.

I struggled to process my Haitian experience. I remembered with a heavy heart the devastating poverty, yet I felt oddly encouraged as I thought about Roxanne's ministry to the women, the dedication of the pastor who protected his rubble, and the young men who were so kind and attentive to us.

I felt like I was leading two lives. One was the ever present memory of that incredible slum where 300,000 Haitians lived in Cite Soleil with tin shacks and mud floors. The other was my comfortable home. *How can I enjoy these comforts when I have seen those who have so little?* I wondered, not expecting the adjustment of being back in the United States to be so hard. I felt deep, internal tension.

Whenever I remembered the day God opened my eyes to the medical needs of the Haitians, I felt the desire to return ignite inside me. As this desire deepened, I spoke with Dale from ARM, exploring the possibility of returning with a medical team. He shared my enthusiasm and began making the arrangements for a trip in October 1989, just six months after our first trip to Haiti. I was ecstatic at the idea of returning.

As Don and I discussed the details of this new trip, we realized that it would not work for Don to join me. We agreed that I should move forward with the plans and he would assist me with the preparations.

I began recruiting for this new team, eagerly telling others about the needs in Haiti. I shared with them my shock when I learned that aspirin is purchased one tablet at a time because a whole bottle would be more than a day's wage. Painting a verbal picture of the poverty was easy as I described the fleas, the garbage and the rustic homes.

It didn't take long before I discovered Donna and Mark, a married couple who were both doctors. They had already spent several weeks serving at a medical clinic in Haiti and were grateful for this opportunity to return to serve the nation that they too had come to love.

Donna and Mark's decision to join the team was the catalyst I needed to push forward. Soon an oral surgeon joined the ranks. I was confident there would be more. Dale recruited several professionals from St Louis to join us, including his wife, Sharon, a nurse. Soon we were a team of twelve, ten with medical training.

There was so much to learn. Since this was a medical team, the trip would be a whole new experience for me. Our lead doctors, Donna and Mark, were good coaches and we were all eager trainees. Their prior experience in Haiti was just what we needed to help us in so many areas, such as collection and packaging of medicines. The doctors and nurses had connections with pharmaceutical representatives who provided free sample packages. As samples are often just a few pills to a package, we met together as a team, repackaging the medicines to reduce the bulk. We also worked to ensure they were packaged properly to meet customs requirements. Spending this time together helped us bond.

Gary, the oral surgeon, would be extracting teeth. He required a generator to provide electricity which would run his equipment. I worried that finding one would be a challenge, but God provided one to the team in St. Louis. It even came with a shipping crate ready for our team to take to Haiti. What an answer to prayer!

Due to the extremity of needs, Donna and Mark prepared us to receive hundreds of patients. The Haitians would be waiting for us each day, many having walked long distances. Each would hope to be chosen to see the doctor.

Our days would begin with the doctors and nurses walking through the crowds, giving "tickets" to those with the most severe symptoms, allowing them to see the doctors. Those with lesser symptoms would see a nurse and be given over-the-counter medications. The prescription medications would be placed in small bags with the appropriate symbols describing the instructions, a moon for those to be taken at night and a sun for those taken in the morning.

We would predetermine how many tickets we could give out by the amount of prescription medicines we had available for each day, but we feared there could be more people than available tickets. If there were enough over-the-counter medications, everyone would at least receive something for their symptoms. We knew that if we ran out, there would be Haitians who had walked great distances with the hope of help, only to be disappointed.

We worried that those sent away could become unruly. As I considered this, I wondered what I would do if I had a sick child who desperately needed the doctor. I would most likely be aggressive for the sake of my child.

What a contrast to my personal experience when seeing a doctor! It was sad and frustrating that so many people were without adequate medical care. Instead of being depressed by the inequalities of life, I rejoiced that I could focus on doing something to bring hope and healing to this one community.

It came as a great shock when Rev. Arboret informed me over the phone that he would be unable to host our team on the dates that we had set. I was devastated by this news after feeling so sure that all the pieces for this team had fallen into place. Now what? Due to the purchase of the airline tickets and the busy schedules of the doctors, I knew we would be unable to move the dates to work around Rev. Arboret's schedule.

While contemplating this dilemma, I considered other organizations in Haiti that could receive a medical team. I began contacting their stateside offices, hoping this would be the solution. However, as each agency explored the request, they informed me the dates would not work for their ministries.

While searching my soul about how this trip had come about, I wondered, *was it just me pushing a good idea, or was I truly called by God to form this team and head back to Haiti?* I was very anxious, knowing the tickets were already purchased.

At this point several people advised me to give up and see this complication as a sign that the team should be canceled. I was confused because I believed that God had spoken to me while I was in Haiti, calling me to return with a medical team. He had a plan for this team and I just needed to hear from Him.

In the past I had learned that the best way for me to sharpen my hearing was to fast. So I gave up food, asking God, *did I really hear you speak to me or was this my own desire?* It was a simple question but had profound implications for me personally. I needed to know if I could trust my instincts; did I actually hear God's leading in Haiti?

After several days of fasting and praying the answer came to me by way of a second unexpected phone call from Rev. Arboret. He was in the United States visiting family in California, and calling to say hello. He was surprised to learn that we were continuing to prepare our team, even though we still had no host to receive us.

To my delight he informed me that his circumstances had changed greatly from the last time we had spoken. He could receive our team after all! He offered to leave immediately, returning to Haiti to prepare for our team's arrival. Finally, God had spoken.

The experience of this roadblock in the path of the team was a good opportunity for me to grow in my understanding of God and how He works. Sometimes we can experience His grace as details come together easily; however, there are times when the roadblocks are there to help us turn our focus to Him. Roadblocks can help us grow in faith, trust and perseverance. In the end I was thankful for this testing and I now was certain with renewed confidence that I had heard God and he was guiding this team.

Roadblocks can help us grow in faith, trust and perseverance.

I returned to the details of team preparations, spending my time exploring the intricacies of guiding a team to and from Haiti. I wanted to learn more about the logistics of preparing teams, connecting with the pastor whom we were going to serve, and working through Customs. I had many conversations with Dale and was grateful that he was eager to teach me. I was energized by the process of making certain all the details were in order so this team could accomplish their task of offering medical assistance to the people. As I helped with preparations I wondered what my role would be once the clinics began. *With no medical expertise to offer, would I fit in?* I did not know.

With less than a week before departure, a local nurse, JoeAnn, called asking if it was possible for her to join the team at this late date. I was surprised by this last minute request. This team had been meeting for several months, learning about the culture, doing Bible studies and building team unity. It did not seem right to allow her to join us because she would not be as prepared. I was wary, but Dale told me if he could get her flights on the same plane, I should welcome her.

That was hard for me. Somehow I thought she didn't deserve to participate since she was not a part of the pre-planning. Then I remembered the Biblical parable about the landowner hiring workers to tend his fields, paying those who started later in the day the same wage as those who worked all day. I realized that I was being exclusive and God wanted me to be inclusive by accepting her as a team member. Surprisingly, all the details for her transportation fell into place. While spending time with JoeAnn during our final packing meeting, I could see that God had provided a very valuable last-minute addition.

The day of departure came. I handled all of the logistics for everyone traveling from Ann Arbor to Port-au-Prince, Haiti. We connected with Dale and the others from St. Louis during the five-hour layover in Miami. Originally, I had wondered what we would do for those hours. I found out. It was during this time that we learned our generator was too heavy and did not meet international airline requirements for baggage. We soon realized that the wooden crate that housed the generator was the problem.

It seemed like an impossible task to dismantle and then reconstruct the crate, but our creative team leader and several team members (with lots of sweat and prayers) accomplished the impossible. They finished just in time to check it in for our flight to Haiti. They were under tremendous pressure, working against a deadline with makeshift tools and only limited space to execute the task. God knew we would need every minute in Miami.

Thankfully, it was an uneventful flight and the generator and bags arrived safely with us in Port-au-Prince. I began the process of assisting Dale in getting everybody and everything through immigration. Dale was a great mentor, and I actually enjoyed the process of moving the thirteen team members and thirty-eight bags plus the generator through the chaotic customs procedure.

While regrouping outside the building, we were greeted by Rev. Arboret and the joyful singing of a choir from one of his local churches. They presented each of us with a bouquet. It was a royal welcome for tired and weary travelers. Once again, I knew I was in Haiti by the smell of burning charcoal. It was good to be back.

We watched as the duffel bags were piled high in the back of two pickup trucks. I wondered how the team would be transported, but soon a van appeared. After an hour of driving, we arrived at Rev. Arboret's home. Jamine welcomed me with a big hug and "Bonjour sister Gayle, Jezi renmen ou." (Jesus loves you). I melted into her embrace.

Although we were exhausted, we were grateful for the time we spent with Rev. Arboret that evening learning more about his ministry over the past several decades. We were surprised by how vast it was. I knew he was passionate about planting churches, a gifted evangelist, and the founder and Bishop of Ebenezer Church of God, but I didn't know he now oversaw over 400 churches, 120 schools, and forty dispensaries that were training young girls in first aid. I felt honored to work with him on this medical team.

We were glad when the day finally ended. We headed to our cots, hoping for a good night's sleep. During our preparations I had warned my team members that our two canine friends, Strength and Protection, would be on duty. As predicted, their strong voices were relentlessly heard, keeping us safe throughout the night.

Morning came too soon. The duffel bags of medicine and all our personal bags were loaded in the van and on the trucks for our trip to Petit Goave, the old orphanage where the team had stayed during the previous visit. We were told we would stop at a pharmaceutical lab on our way to Petit Goave to get deworming medicine. It was expected that most of the patients would need this medicine since intestinal worms are endemic to Haiti.

The stop for the extra medication put us in the heart of the capital city, and also close to Cite Soleil. I was elated when we stopped for a brief visit to see the church that I held so dear to my heart from my first team. What a joy it was to be welcomed by the pastor and the members of the church. It was so encouraging to see that the church was now complete.

It was the rainy season in Haiti. Water was everywhere. The standing garbage in March was now the floating garbage in October. My heart broke as I thought about living in these tin huts with dirt floors that flooded. I also noticed that the church, with its new raised foundation, stood proudly above the water. I was moved as I thought about the wisdom of the pastor and his selfless sacrifice as he slept there for so many nights guarding that rubble. The debris that we had been ready to throw away now provided the base for this raised floor, offering a refuge for those around it.

My heart broke as I thought about living in these tin huts with dirt floors that flooded.

It was a thrill for me to enter the church through a proper door and to be greeted by the 'Allelu' banner we had presented to them, now hanging on the wall behind the pulpit. I tried to explain to the team members what a profound renovation had occurred since our previous team had been there, but felt my words were inadequate to truly convey the transformation.

I realized that the church was not the only thing transformed by the last team. The transformation in me was just as profound. I had been changed, returning home with new insights regarding poverty, myself and God. I was grateful that Rev. Arboret provided this brief visit to see the church, the pastor and his wife. It gave me great peace, knowing that now, with restored walls and a strong locked door; the faithful pastor could sleep at home with his family.

We continued to Petit Goave, where we would be staying. Bad roads and no shock absorbers on the buses made for another long bumpy ride. I never knew my rib cage could ache so much from bouncing up and down on a well-worn seat.

We stopped to visit the future site of our medical clinic. It was smaller than expected. It was going to be a challenge to convert this small twenty-by-thirty foot church building into five examination rooms for the doctors and oral surgeon, plus an area for the pharmacy. We discussed where we would hang the sheets to create the divisions for the small examining rooms and how the patients would flow through this temporary clinic.

When we learned that Rev. Arboret used the radio stations to announce the clinic, we became very concerned about the crowds that would arrive at that small building. The church was on a major bus route, and with that kind of radio advertising and easy access we could easily be overwhelmed.

We continued the drive to Petit Goave, unpacked all the bags of medicines and prepared them for distribution at the clinic. When I saw the mountain of medicine come out of the duffels and suitcases, I knew God had big plans for our team. It had been a long day, but my spirits were high as I sorted medicines, knowing that soon we would be helping relieve many Haitians' pain and suffering. I could hardly wait to get started.

After the sorting we gathered for a team meeting where we were introduced to Rev. Arboret's daughter Gladys, a nurse, her husband Roland, a pastor, and their friend, Dr. Phillip. All of them were joining our team.

Initially, our discussions focused on crowd control, knowing the size of the building would present many challenges. The most interesting aspect of that meeting, however, was when the Haitians began teaching us about the local voodoo beliefs and how they feared it could interfere with our efforts. They explained that it was essential for us to understand how the Haitians think and how this might affect the medical team members' ability to accurately diagnose their patients.

We were surprised to learn that the Haitian society practiced "concealment," meaning that questions regarding health issues or family matters were often not answered directly. The motivation for this was fear. Fear that by speaking about personal information the evil spirits would hear them and with that knowledge cause them harm. Fear that speaking these answers out loud could also result in providing personal information to anyone who was listening. Fear, then, that this information could be used against them. With personal knowledge one could ask a witch doctor to cast a spell on their neighbor or family member, hoping to bring them illness or any other manner of difficulties.

We learned that a typical exam could sound like this:

Doctor: What is your trouble?
Patient: I spit blood last night
Doctor: How long have you been ill?
Patient: The other day
Doctor: How many days?
Patient: Not a long time.
Doctor: Can't you tell me how many days?
Patient: I spit blood last night.
Doctor: Do you have a fever?
Patient: Sometimes.
Doctor: Do you have it with this illness?
Patient: Not now.

The effects of the voodoo beliefs penetrated deeper than we had expected. It was certainly going to create a challenge for the doctors and nurses, but it was good that they were now aware and could adjust their questioning. Sadly, we feared that the voodoo practices and beliefs could work against the good the medical team hoped to accomplish.

I was grateful to learn that Jamine would be there to share her faith with all who came through the clinic. Jamine's heart burned

> *The effects of the voodoo beliefs penetrated deeper than we had expected.*

for her countrymen, knowing that accepting Christ would free her Haitian brothers and sisters from this life of fear. By having the medical clinic at the church, we hoped it would open doors for her to invite them to return to learn more about a loving Savior.

I was looking forward to the first day of the clinic, but with all the concerns for crowd control, voodoo beliefs, and the typical Haitian night noises, it was hard to relax. I lay awake, praying for our team and the Haitians. I marveled at God's gift to me that day, the surprise visit to Cite Soleil where I witnessed the completed church and stood in the place where I had first felt the desire to bring medical help to Haiti, just six months earlier. It was hard to comprehend how quickly my desire had become a reality, confirming again that this was God's plan. With that knowledge, I wondered what tomorrow would hold as I anticipated the medical clinic.

6

Lessons Learned

No matter how well one prepares, there are always circumstances that can take precedence over the best-laid plans. Unfortunately, my first day of our Haitian medical clinic began with such circumstances. I was not well.

Several others were experiencing the same symptoms and it seemed that we were reacting to something we ate or simply battling the effects of travel. We were grateful for the indoor plumbing, but very disappointed that we needed to remain at the pastor's home, unable to assist in the first day of clinic. We needed to spend the day resting and staying hydrated in order to recover and rejoin the team.

That evening when the other team members returned, we learned that it had been an amazing first day. Even with several of us ill, they were able to successfully treat 300 people. As wonderful as that news was, we also knew that we had come prepared to serve a total of 600 people in three days of clinic. Now half of our medicines were already gone. We had no choice but to fully restock the suitcases that were used to dispense the medicines at the clinic site, and pray that we would be able to continue to meet everyone's needs for the next two days.

When morning arrived, I was glad to have recovered and eager to find my place in serving the people. It had been hard for me to stay back; I wanted to be on the front lines of ministry.

Just as we expected, the team arrived at the clinic site to be greeted by hundreds of hopeful Haitians. The wire fence in front of the church had been draped with colorful banners with Bible verses made by the

Haitian church members, proclaiming a God who loves, a Christian witness in a land dark with voodoo.

The first event of the day was an opening prayer with all who were waiting. Then the doctors and nurses circulated through the large crowd of sick people, quickly assessing which individuals were the most critical and would receive the "tickets" to see the doctors. The others were considered the outpatients. Their most common complaints were fever, stomachache, sore throat, and diarrhea. They received the over-the-counter medicines. Overall, everything was running as smoothly as could be expected in the exhausting circumstances caused by the intense heat, crowds, and noisy generator.

When I was preparing for the trip, I had wondered what my role would be during the clinics. I assumed there would be many ways I could help. Now, with no medical training and having missed the first day, I was struggling to find where I fit. I tried to be useful, but was often unsuccessful, at times even feeling like I was in the way.

Seeing that there were long lines of people waiting for prescriptions, I had tried to be helpful in the pharmacy, but that didn't seem to work out for me. While searching to find my niche at the clinic, I experienced this overwhelming sense that I was extra baggage and the team would be better off if I had not come. I struggled to keep a positive attitude.

Having brought several hundred donated youth toothbrushes, I decided this could be a good time to hand them out. However, what started out peacefully soon turned into a riot of young boys encircling me, pushing aggressively as they tried to take the box from my hands. Frightened, I was caught off guard. Fortunately, a Haitian adult who witnessed the scene rescued me. This, of course, just made me feel even more useless; I could not even manage a simple task of dispensing toothbrushes.

It was a hard day for me. At the day's end I was glad to be back on the bus, yet painfully aware that everyone was enthusiastically talking about their day's experiences. What could I say? I had contributed nothing, and even caused a small riot!

Although I had felt inadequate, the day had been a great success for the clinic. During the evening devotions we were encouraged when we realized that we had served 450 people that day and still had medicine left over. We should have run out, but had not. We praised God and reckoned that there was some heavenly math occurring, like the biblical multiplication of the loaves and the fishes.

...we realized that we had served 450 people that day and still had medicine left over.

We also enjoyed hearing from Jamine as she would share with us about the people with whom she had prayed. She was so compassionate and faithful in her desire to bring Christ to each person.

The next day I woke up feeling ill again, but decided I could go to the clinic. Unfortunately, on this final day of clinic, everyone's nerves seemed to be on edge. The fatigue was beginning to set in as the lines of people seemed to grow longer instead of shorter. We tried singing and praising God and praying to overcome the oppression and the difficulties we were encountering.

Then the rains came, a heavy downpour. The people outside tried to force their way into an already overcrowded clinic. Some children were even in danger of being crushed against the door! Just as we had feared, there were times when it was hard to keep the crowds under control. Fortunately, JoeAnn had a way of working with the crowds, bringing order through her calm demeanor. I thanked God that He had added her to our team.

Despite the struggles we were facing, God was at work in a mighty way. That day a sixteen-year-old frightened boy arrived at the clinic in a wheelbarrow pushed by his father. He had been hit by a car a week earlier and the Haitian hospitals, requiring that the patient pay for services before they are treated, refused him when they learned his parents had no money. He arrived with an eye that would not focus and so much pain in his body that he would not allow anyone to touch him. He was tense and frightened, but Dr. Phillip encouraged him to relax, allowing him to examine his leg and eye.

After much prayer by the doctors, we watched in amazement as he left walking with only a slight sprained ankle. Only God knows what internal and emotional injuries were healed that day to allow such a transformation. I was moved as I watched him leave, pushing the wheelbarrow in which he had arrived.

Another amazing miracle occurred with a little girl who had one leg that was several inches too short, due to a birth deformity. Our Haitian doctor, having compassion for her and knowing medicines could not heal her, prayed with her, asking God to grow her leg.

...I watched him leave, pushing the wheel barrow in which he had arrived.

It did, growing to be a perfect match!

I was not there to witness this miracle, but many team members and Haitians were. I had noticed her, when she arrived at the clinic. She clearly walked with a limp. Now, she was walking with a perfect gait—not even a hint of a limp!

I watched her leave and wondered what the people in her village would think when they witnessed her walk so well. What a testimony she would be to God's power and compassion, a power much stronger than their voodoo gods! Her village would now see the good works of a God of love, not fear.

Infected sores were scrubbed clean, antibiotics given and pain relieved. Many, many people were grateful to have rotten teeth pulled or an abscess in the mouth cleaned and drained. Despite their struggle with heat and exhaustion, the team saw that God was ever present in the healing process.

One patient had a large tumor on the back of his neck; it was the size of an orange, forcing his head forward so he could only look downward. After much discussion among the doctors, it was decided the tumor could be removed with a simple surgery. He and his wife were given bus fare to go to our lodgings where the doctors would perform the surgery that evening.

God's hand was also present as the generator began to sputter towards dark. There was no more gas available for it. The team prayed that the Lord would multiply the gas until the last patient was seen and we would no longer need the lights. Miraculously, it ran for another ninety minutes until the clinic was over.

Although I was aware of all of the amazing miracles, I was still struggling with the very strong feeling that I did not have a purpose on this team. As this final day at the clinic came to an end, I determined that my contribution could be helping to dissemble the clinic. After all, I was tall and could easily reach the tops of the bed sheets that were hanging as room dividers. I found a chair that I could stand on and waited for the word that our clinic was closed.

I stood on that chair, only to be told to "step down and let me do that" by one of the men. I could not convince him that I wanted to do it myself. He was sure he was doing me a favor. My only hope for feeling useful was now shattered; I was left with more defeat and another bus ride back, listening to everyone's exclamations about their day, intensifying my defeat.

As I sat there on the bus, I wondered how many times in my life I had been insensitive to the need of others around me to feel useful. Bouncing along the bumpy road to the orphanage gave me plenty of time to reflect, trying to determine if God was teaching me to be a more sensitive leader or if God was telling me my talents lay in recruiting and training team members that could go to serve in Haiti without me. That thought almost brought me to tears since I longed to be in Haiti. I continued to dwell on this as we arrived back at our team lodging, knowing that our day's work was still not over.

Our patient with the tumor on his neck had arrived, waiting for the surgery that was promised to him. After supper we cleared off the dining table which was a large piece of plywood on sawhorses covered with a plastic tablecloth. Now that same table was transformed into an operating table. Even though everyone was exhausted, the doctors dutifully scrubbed, preparing for this event.

After supper we cleared off the dining table...now that same table was transformed into an operating table.

It was 11:00 p.m. when sterile sheets were placed on the plywood table along with sterile surgical tools. It was fascinating to watch the process unfold. The patient was given a local anesthetic and Dr. Mark began the surgery. I had never witnessed such precision and care. All this happened on the dinner table in a very dark room with one bright bare light bulb hanging down from the ceiling.

My job was to whisk the flies that were drawn to the open wound away from the patient during the surgery. I finally felt useful. Once the surgery was completed, we cleaned up and headed to bed, too tired to really contemplate all that had taken place on that last day of clinic. We all slept well that night.

The next morning we could see that the surgery was a huge success. The wound was healing well and the patient could now, for the first time in fifteen years, hold his head up, a transformed man. As he and his wife prepared to leave, they gave us grateful hugs with tears of joy streaming down their faces.

Our team had successfully completed the three days of clinics and now came together to enjoy our leisurely morning devotions. There was great camaraderie among the team members, sharing their experiences from the last three days. It was an awkward time for me, though, since I had little to contribute. As the devotions progressed, one of the men from St. Louis shared some Bible verses God had put on his heart about how we are all important members of the body of Christ. He related that to our team and how uniquely every team member was valued as they contributed toward the team ministry.

During our time of prayer this nagging thought kept coming to me, *"everyone but you has value."* I finally recognized it was more than just a thought; it was the voice of Satan. Humbly I realized I needed to share my struggles with this team.

They were shocked, and encouraged me by sharing that they saw me as a strong competent leader, always available when needed. They reminded me of the positive role I had played on this team: from recruiting and preparing the team to leading them through customs. The members shared how they appreciated not needing to worry about those details so that they could focus on what they came to do—provide medical care to the Haitians.

This devotion, and my willingness to be vulnerable by sharing my feelings, helped bring healing to my wounded soul. I was able to reclaim my worth through Christ and deny Satan the ability to feed me such lies. Now I could see the truth—that I was a unique and valuable part of this team as well as the body of Christ.

After the encouraging words from my team members, I began to see that maybe this medical team had been "God's Boot Camp" for me. Boot camp is known for being very demanding on recruits, training them to listen and obey their commanders. I had allowed myself to listen to Satan's lies and needed to be reminded that *my* general in command was my Lord and Savior, Jesus Christ. I rejoiced at His grace and compassion.

As I leaned back in my seat feeling the familiar lift of our plane as it began our ascent towards home, I closed my eyes and considered all that God had taught me on this team:

I learned to seek God for His direction and not be influenced by circumstances such as when Rev. Arboret originally cancelled the medical team. This obstacle became an opportunity for a deeper relationship with God and renewed my confidence in listening to that small inner voice that I believed I heard when in Cite Soleil.

I learned to be inclusive and not exclusive. I didn't want to add a last minute team member because I didn't think JoeAnn deserved to benefit from all our prior planning, but God knew I needed to welcome her wholeheartedly and not reluctantly. He chose her and I needed to choose her also. He knew she would be a valuable team member.

I learned that painful experiences can have a positive outcome. I planned to be a more sensitive leader in the future, making sure everyone has a useful role on any future mission trips.

I learned to discern who was influencing my thoughts. While listening to a fallen angel who told me I was worthless, I believed his lies and suffered the consequences. Allowing myself to be vulnerable and sharing my insecurities with my team members enabled them to encourage me, redirecting my focus to the one true God, restoring my self-worth. No one is worthless in God's eyes.

I also learned that my presence on the team as a leader contributed to the success of the team, even when I was fighting an internal battle.

As I watched the familiar outline of the Haitian island fade away, I reflected on the common Christian saying: "God does not call the equipped, but equips the called." God was certainly equipping me!

I was humbled as I considered how God was using me, especially as I remembered my past. There are no secrets from God. He knew how, as a young married woman, I had once questioned His existence and turned my back on Him.

7

Is God Real?

Back in college, after feeling God had confirmed that I should "*marry Don Sommerfeld*," Don and I began to plan our life together. It was spring of 1957 and Don and I still had two more years of schooling. Attending classes and paying for college were our top priorities.

When we considered our combined scholarships, we soon realized that we could easily pay for our tuition, an apartment together and books. With that good news we planned an August wedding. We were married in the beautiful Lutheran Chapel by Don's father, a Lutheran pastor. After a brief honeymoon we settled down in our new apartment and looked forward to our classes.

As the semester began, we realized we had not received my scholarship check. Bills were piling up. When the envelope finally arrived, there was no check. Instead it contained a letter denying me my scholarship. It was their policy not to support married women! Several phone calls to the scholarship board were futile. I was frustrated over the obvious injustice—men could marry and keep their scholarships, but not women.

The hardships that followed took their toll on us. We always carried a maximum load of credits and now we had to get jobs. It was difficult, but I would not give up my dream. I had recently changed majors and was excited to be studying Sociology, the study of society and culture. A perfect fit for my interests in people and ethnic groups.

After a year and a half of juggling work and school, we were exhausted. We decided rather than increase our student loans we would take a break from school and focus on work. We moved to Holland, Michigan, where we each found jobs and enjoyed reconnecting with my many cousins.

Six months later, life took another unexpected turn. I was pregnant! I was overwhelmed because I had not considered a family, but only dreamed of college and adventures. After much prayer and discussion Don and I decided that we should try to finish our degrees before the baby arrived. With that decision made, we packed up and moved back to Illinois and purchased an old trailer home near the university's campus.

As I unpacked, I found myself reflecting on my mother and the strength she had shown during her many challenges. I remembered the words from her favorite hymn and imagined God walking with Don and me as we returned to our schooling and prepared for our baby.

Little did I know that I would soon doubt the faith that had brought me such comfort.

With a sociology major and philosophy minor, I had a full load of courses that fed my appetite for knowledge. I was not prepared, however, for the spiritual challenge I faced in my World Religions class.

On the first day, the professor asked, "Who in this class is a Christian?" Out of the 200 students present, only three of us raised our hands.

I have vivid memories of the professor's animated lectures describing the religious beliefs and practices of cultures from around the world. Just as he was describing some bizarre belief and I was thinking, *how can anyone believe that?*, he would interject how that particular idea mirrored one of my own Christian beliefs. I was shocked. Most of the student body was amused and laughed at his analogy.

It wasn't long before I was feeling confused and deeply troubled. With each lecture my personal belief system was being shattered. I became concerned. It seemed that there were just too many broken pieces for me to put it all back into a nice neat little package called faith. I was filled with questions and doubts.

Is there one God, many gods, or no God at all? These questions loomed large in my soul. *Who was I talking to as I knelt before my bed as a child? Was there a God out there that cared and listened to me?* I had always felt such a deep desire to pray and talk to God, as my mother had. *Was she wrong? Was it just a coping mechanism or a crutch?*

I was confused. I had never questioned my faith before. Now, how was I to go forward without God?

On the last day of class, the professor repeated his question, "Who in this class is a Christian?" My hands remained in my lap. Gone was the confidence I possessed on that first day. So it was for the other students. No one claimed to be a Christian.

While struggling internally with faith issues, I made sure that on the outside everything appeared normal as I continued to attend the chapel where we were married. I was afraid to speak to Don about my crisis of faith. He seemed so sure of his beliefs. I did not want him to doubt as I was doubting or for him to be disappointed in me.

I could not dwell long on these upsetting questions because my daily schedule was demanding with studying, term papers, and exams. I was also getting ready for our child.

Our new baby, Scott, was born just after my spring term exams. Don and I were excited and overwhelmed as we added this new little person into our lives. Don graduated that spring, and I graduated that summer. One of my favorite pictures is of our adorable new addition, Scott, propped up on the couch between both Don's and my diplomas.

As we looked for employment, we chose to head back to the Chicago area. We moved our trailer to a suburb, not too far from my parents who could assist with the care of Scott. Don commuted downtown by train for work and I enjoyed working in an office in the local community.

I continued to question God's existence, but still did not share my doubts with Don. We attended a large church. I considered it more like a country club than a place of worship, enjoying the social gatherings with couples our age. The pastor preached inspiring sermons and I admired his intellect, wondering how he could believe what he preached. I never did ask.

Eventually, the issue of God's existence weighed so heavily on my spirit that I could not avoid it anymore. Life without God was empty and purposeless. One day, while vacuuming the well-worn carpet in our trailer home, I agonized over my unresolved faith issues.

My intellectual pursuits regarding God had been futile, spinning me in many directions. I began to wonder if my intellect, although great in my own eyes, was just not sufficient to understand God. I remembered Isaiah 55:8 where God declares, "As the heavens are higher than the earth, so are my ways higher than your ways and my thoughts than your thoughts." I began to wonder, w*as it arrogant of me to think that I could fully grasp and understand God?*

...was it arrogant of me to think that I could fully grasp and understand God?

I finally surrendered my pride, and asked God to reveal himself to me. I wanted to believe again. In that moment God took charge. I felt an inner peace and a certainty that He exists. I was able to believe *in* Him and surrender to His will once again. I felt as though I was a prodigal daughter, returning to her beloved Father. With vacuum in hand I realized that this well-worn carpet had become hallowed ground as I basked in the assurance that God did indeed exist!

8

Unmet Expectations

After leading two teams to Haiti, God was helping me to recognize the woes of my reactions to "unmet expectations." My frustration when an event did not unfold as I expected could cloud my ability to see what He might have in store.

On this past medical team to Haiti I was guilty of once again desiring my own way. I had not realized it, but I had gone on this team with an expectation that I would feel useful, giving me a sense of purpose. When it did not happen, I focused on myself, taking my eyes off of God. This robbed me of the very joy He had in store for me.

God was continuing to teach me to let go of my expectations and to trust Him in all circumstances. I was learning that the act of "letting go and letting God" would be a lifelong lesson for me, requiring me to daily surrender and refocus on Him.

All of my experiences seemed to be adding up to help equip me, giving me insight into how to follow God's will and surrender my own. I could also see that these lessons were preparing me for future short-term mission teams. I knew that if there were to be any more teams, we would discuss at great lengths the need for all team members to let go of preconceived expectations, doing our best to enter the mission field with an open mind, allowing God to lead and reveal His plan for each of us.

I thanked God that Don and I did not get trapped in the guilt and depression that often occurs after witnessing extreme poverty. Instead, God filled us with joy and hope. We were motivated by the words of

Proverbs 3:27, "Do not withhold good from those that deserve it, when it is in your power to act." We felt that with our new connections in Haiti and interest in teams, it was within our power to help these Haitians. We knew that God was clearly calling us to act.

While I was away on the Haitian medical team, Don spent his time focusing on researching and writing grants for the various Haitian projects previously discussed with Rev. Arboret. He explored the grant for the fishing cooperative, hoping to help provide food for the local community. Don also looked into what it would take to design an inexpensive metal bunk bed that could be used in the tin huts, helping more family members to have a safe place to sleep during the rainy seasons. Thankfully, the grant for the fishing boat was awarded, however the one for the beds was not.

After I returned home, I continued to serve the Haitians by collecting gently used shoes. I had noticed their tattered shoes, often held together with tape or string. Posting a notice with pictures of their well-worn footwear on the church bulletin board, I hoped to inspire the members of our congregation to donate their gently used shoes.

Shortly after posting the request, I was approached by a businesswoman who offered me more than 200 pairs of new men's leather shoes. She worked for a company that was going out of business and needed to dispose of their inventory immediately! I stood in awe as she spoke; *Lord, did she really just say they needed to get rid of more than 200 pairs of brand new shoes?* How incredible! This was no coincidence; it was clear to me that God had orchestrated this timing. God was working here—just as He had in Haiti.

My concern for the Haitians drew me closer to God. He revealed to me in greater clarity my part in His plans. I marveled at how God had orchestrated meeting both the needs in Haiti and needs of the shoe company. I was unsure how the shoes would find their way to Haiti, but was confident that God would solve that problem in His own time.

> Lord, did she just say they needed to get rid of more than 200 brand new shoes?

Just as Don and I were consumed with thoughts of Haiti, the other medical team members also returned to the States enthusiastically sharing about their experiences. Word spread among the hospital staff as Mark and Donna told their colleagues about the great needs of the Haitian people. They shared how our small team saw 1,500 patients in three days of clinics, how the medicines miraculously multiplied, and the many medical miracles that occurred. They also shared with their Christian coworkers about Jamine and how important it was that she ministered to the spiritual needs of the people. After hearing the stories, several people asked if they could also join a medical mission team to Haiti.

After talking with Donna and Mark and hearing their interest in returning, I contacted Dale. He was just as eager and suggested that we begin making preparations to leave in a few months. I paused as I hung up the phone: *Really Lord? Are you calling us back so soon?*

As excited as I was, I knew Don and I could not join. We no longer had the needed funds available after paying for three round trip tickets in six months. I also did not want to assume that it was God's intention for me to join this team. I ached to return, but was also confident that I could assist the team from home.

I was surprised when I received a phone call from Dale stating that the team members were expressing hesitancy in making the trip without me. Several of the doctors had shared that they did not want to do any of the administration of the team while in Haiti; it would be a distraction from their medical efforts. Dale, knowing finances were the largest stumbling block, made a very generous offer. ARM would pay for the airfare for both Don and me. Overwhelmed by their generosity we eagerly accepted.

I pulled out my pen and well-worn journal, I was developing a deeper understanding of the words in Psalm 37:4, "Take delight in the Lord, and He will give you the desires of your heart." *I do delight in you, Lord, seeking to love and honor you each day. Thank you,* I penned, *for placing this desire within me to love and serve the Haitians and now granting me the ability to act on this desire!*

Plans were set. We would leave in February, only a few months away. Our invitation for this medical clinic was to serve the island of La Gonave, an island that was governed by Haiti and considered even poorer than the mainland.

Many years ago, undesirables, the criminals, the sick, and the elderly were sent to the island of La Gonave from the mainland. They were left to fend for themselves on top of a rugged mountain with no sanitation or clean water nearby. We learned that the only medical clinic on the island was at the base of the mountain and that most of the islanders were unable to make the trek. Many of the islanders would never have the opportunity to leave this small island. With very few schools, there was little hope of reducing their poverty.

Knowing that Rev. Arboret had 127 schools throughout Haiti, I wondered if he might have a school on this island. I had a special interest in his school ministry. After my first team to Haiti my brother, Gordon, had listened intently to the story regarding the school that needed help feeding it's students. Visibly concerned and feeling inspired to help Haitian children, Gordon asked for help in contacting Rev. Arboret. I later learned that he had become a benefactor for several schools.

It was exciting for me to see how our love for the Haitians was extending beyond Don and me. It was like that first trip was a little drop in a lake, where the rippling effects continued extending out, through individuals like Gordon, beyond what we could see.

Rev. Arboret did have schools on this island and we were informed that the location for the clinic would be in one of his schools. How surprised I was to learn that the name of the school was "Breuker Ecole" (Breuker School), one of the schools my brother, Gordon Breuker, was supporting! It was heartwarming to think of a school in Haiti with my maiden name.

As I was putting together this new team, I realized that the delivery problem for the new shoes was solved. This medical team to La Gonave could transport and deliver those 200 pairs of new shoes to Rev. Arboret. It was wonderful to see that God was making sure those shoes would get to His people in Haiti.

All seemed to be falling into place until Dale called, informing us that he would no longer be able to participate. Thankfully, his wife Sharon, who was on the first medical team, would still be joining us.

With this news I realized that I would need to carry out many of Dale's team leader responsibilities and was glad that on the previous teams he had spent time mentoring me. He reassured me that he felt confident in my abilities and would help with the preparations.

Considering this change of events, I wondered if this was God confirming the recurring idea I had been having: *Lord, are you preparing me to be a leader of short-term mission teams?* I loved the thought of returning to Haiti with more teams, and believed that desire came from God. Energized and excited, I considered that this could be the beginning of a new short-term mission ministry led by Don and me.

The planning and preparing for this new team was easier since many of us were experienced. I made sure we included discussions on the importance of keeping an open mind and being emotionally flexible. We discussed how to respond to the frustrations and distractions experienced when there are unmet expectations out on the mission field. We also prepared everyone for the very real reverse culture shock experienced when reentering the United States.

The island of La Gonave offered new challenges. There would be no building to house us. We were to bring our own tents and bedding. Don and I purchased a new spacious tent and borrowed an air mattress. It would not provide the comforts of the previous trips, but it would be adequate.

Once in Haiti we were welcomed again by the familiar smell of burning charcoal and the sounds of the musicians. As we made our way through customs, I was concerned, as the leader of our team, that the officials might confiscate the duffle bags filled with shoes. Would they be tempted to take the shoes for themselves? Thankfully, they took little notice and sent us on our way.

The trip to the island was made in a large, wooden boat. There were no seats and we found ourselves balancing on the boat's edge as we swayed back and forth under the brilliant sun. The belly of the boat was filled with our many duffel bags of medications, tents, and enough beans and rice to feed the forty individuals, both Haitian and American, needed to carry out our three days of clinic.

When we reached the shore, we faced a long, uphill trip to the top of a steep and rugged mountain, where our clinic would be located. While the team bounced along in the bed of a land rover, our gear was carried on the backs of donkeys. I was thankful when the exhausting day of travel and clinic preparations ended.

In the evening all forty of us gathered around the fire, singing and praising God. The stress of the day slowly began to melt away as I listened to the Haitians sing worship songs. Closing my eyes, I allowed their music to surround me, turning my heart toward God and thanking Him for bringing me back here once again and to the people whom I was so drawn.

After the singing, we had a time of prayer. The local pastor's wife shared that she longed to have children, but had been unable to conceive. Her emotional pain was evident as she asked us to join her in prayers that God would grant her a family.

As the evening came to a close, I was brought back to reality as I remembered that Don and I had been asked to offer our brand new five-person tent to some Haitian helpers. We had been given a smaller two-person pup tent. We had to crawl into it, and the ceiling was so low we couldn't sit up! Disappointed, I reminded myself of my recent lessons on the destruction that frustrations over unmet expectations can create. Yes, I had expected to share a spacious new tent with Don, but I now had the chance to try to let go of those ideas, and accept my new circumstances.

The next day, I woke up on hard, rocky ground. Our borrowed air mattress had sprung a leak! It was becoming more difficult to let go of my expectations of physical comfort. I did not enjoy the thought that we would be spending the remainder of the trip sleeping on the ground without a buffer.

Tired and frustrated, but trying to be emotionally flexible as God seemed to be teaching me, I wriggled out of our tent. When I had exited successfully, I looked around. Hundreds of Haitian eyes stared back. The people had surrounded our camp, waiting silently and patiently for us to wake up. I quickly returned to my tent, changing my clothing as well as my attitude. I praised God that I could be there, offering hope to those Haitians, who had few expectations regarding physical comfort.

I quickly returned to my tent, changing my clothing as well as my attitude.

The day went well. Our greatest stress was crowd control. Although the Haitians had begun the day waiting patiently, it soon became a challenge to keep the crowd from trying to push their way into the clinic. Wisely, we moved the waiting area further down the mountain, away from the clinic. Don also had a plan. He brought a set of juggling balls to entertain the crowds as they waited. They loved it!

The Haitian evangelist circled through the crowd. She encouraged them to give up their voodoo fetishes and turn to the one true God. Initially she was treated with cool suspicion, but as each day wore on, the mood changed. Small crowds formed around her, listening intently as she shared her faith. Some even asked her for advice.

Through the creativity of a team member, our air mattress was patched. I was thankful the mattress still had some air left in it when I woke up on the third day. The morning was routine: a cup of water to use for a sponge bath, followed by a delicious breakfast of black beans and rice. I never seemed to tire of the many ways they prepared this nutritious combination.

After our morning prayers we began the clinic with triage. It went quicker this time, with the doctors and nurses swiftly moving among those who were waiting. Selecting the sickest was the easiest task when it was obvious. Open wounds and those with high fevers were easy to see. It became easier to ignore those who were faking pain or exaggerating their condition. Children who were listless were given priority tickets.

An eighteen-year-old mother of five brought her twin daughter and son to the clinic. They were barely responsive. The twins were suffering from a severe case of malnutrition and dehydration. The infants appeared to be about four months old, but actually were ten months. They were lethargic, and their condition caused all of us great concern. With no bottles to be found we wondered how we could save them.

It was wonderful to watch the doctors as they creatively fashioned a bottle out of an empty vitamin bottle and the finger of a surgical glove, poking a hole in the tip to serve as the nipple. Don and I took those very listless twins and held them on our laps. Our only instructions were to keep them sucking on the special fluid until they urinated, a sure sign that they were rehydrated. We each had one on our lap, waiting for the time when their gaunt look would change to smiles. They loved the rehydration fluid, and sucked eagerly on that surgical glove nipple. After several hours we were able to shout with joy...it was time for a diaper change!

The team could provide the mother with the nourishing baby formula needed, but feared that in her desperate circumstances, she would sell it. It was decided that the mother was to bring the twins daily to the local pastor's home for the feedings. I taught the pastor's wife how to make a baby bottle with the glove and how to prepare the formula. Although they were not her own babies, she was thankful to have this unique opportunity to nurture these children. We found out later that the young mother eventually gave the pastor and his wife her twins to raise. It was a unique, and unexpected, answer to their prayers for a family!

As the clinic was nearing its end, I asked for an interpreter to assist me in talking to the schoolteachers. Since we were using their building, the school children met at a temporary site, under a thatched roof made from palm fronds. The walls were a combination of woven mats and the bed sheets we brought. I was glad to see that this school had benches and the children were not sitting on mats on the ground as is common in the poorer schools. Most of the children were in uniform, a cotton blouse or shirt with skirts or pants for the boys. Uniforms are provided since most of the children are too poor to have the proper dress to attend school. I was amazed at how clean every child was—and wondered what effort was necessary to wash those uniforms when the water was far away.

As I watched the children stare at me, I realized that on this remote island it was quite possible that these children had never seen a white person before. Looking at their solemn faces I wondered what they were thinking; after all we had displaced them from their school.

The teachers were young women who had graduated from the National School. All subjects were taught, including geography. They asked if I could talk to my brother, Gordon, about sending maps. The teachers wished to show the children how to find Haiti and the United States of America. I agreed.

Over the course of the three days of clinics, the team was successful in ministering to nearly a thousand Haitians. We were also instrumental in saving the life of a pregnant woman suffering from a ruptured tubal pregnancy. Once stabilized, she had been loaded onto the bed of a truck and transported to the hospital at the bottom of the mountain. I watched as they pulled away, her frail body lying on an inflatable mattress. A nurse knelt beside her, holding her IV bag. It was a solemn thought to consider that she would have certainly died had we not been there to provide the care and transportation.

The three days of clinics passed quickly. Exhausted but satisfied, most of the team was quiet as we boarded the boat. Thoughts of adjusting to home once again filled my mind as I watched the island recede.

At home, I knew it was important to share with my friends and family who prayed for us how God had answered their prayers and done so much more than we had even hoped. I wrote a letter and in it I concluded with the retelling of a familiar adaptation of a story originally written by Loren Eiseley. I hoped it conveyed how I felt about each team to Haiti, and my motivation to return:

The Star Thrower

A boy was walking along a beach, throwing objects into the ocean. "What are you doing?" an old man asks the boy.

"These starfish have washed ashore and if they don't get back into the water, they will die" the boy says, pointing to the thousands of starfish lying stranded.

The man replied, "You'll never be able to save them all, so what does it matter?"

The boy looks at the starfish in his hand. "Well, sir" he says as he throws that starfish into the waves, "It matters to this one."

We were trying to make a difference, one team at a time. Although the needs were great, I knew that what we did mattered to God and to the Haitians we served.

It was not long before I was once again sitting on my comfortable living room couch, pen in hand, journaling my thoughts to God. I had returned to my American life, changed again by my experiences. This time I was not struggling. I was excited. God was revealing His plan for my life: leading teams to Haiti!

I marveled that God had chosen me for this important task and felt humbled as I again considered my past. Not only had I once doubted God's existence, but after I surrendered and regained my faith in God, I had remained surprisingly skeptical of the role of Jesus in my life. I had once even asked: "Do I really need a Savior?" Thankfully, during my early thirties, that question was answered.

9

Knowing Jesus

It was during the late 1960's, several years after I acknowledged the existence of God, that I had stated, "I think I would make a good Jew" to a group of churchwomen as we gathered to study the Bible. "I don't really see the need for Jesus." No one commented. There was an awkward silence before the leader redirected the discussion.

Don and I were living in Ann Arbor, Michigan, where Don had received his Ph.D. in Psychology and Education and was now working full-time. We bought a modest home and were currently raising three children; Scott, Bradley, and Sandra. David, our youngest, would join the family several years later.

I believed in God, even loved and served Him, but I did not understand the need to have a relationship with His Son, Jesus. After all, I had lived my life according to the dictates of my conscience and as best I could tell, I was a good person. I did not feel I needed a Savior.

My personal beliefs were about to be challenged.

After one very stormy church voters meeting where several prominent lay leaders had engaged in a heated name-calling debate, I felt irritated and discouraged with the church at large. I called my sister-in-law, Pat, and shared with her my growing frustrations.

Pat told me about her friend in Ann Arbor who participated in a Christian small group prayer meeting. This group was filled with individuals who belonged to different churches, but met together regularly in homes to worship God and study His Word. I was intrigued. I looked forward to meeting these believers.

When we attended the meeting, I was surprised by the peaceful presence that I felt. It was similar to the time I was vacuuming and God welcomed me into His presence, assuring me of His existence. I listened intently to their intimate prayers of praise. I noticed several people praying genuinely from their hearts, expressing sincere and very personal adoration for their Lord and Savior. They were speaking to Jesus as though they knew him personally. I was not sure how to ·respond.

It was as though I was experiencing the deep faith I had read about in the life of the early Christians in the book of Acts, but this was twenty centuries later! My confidence that I did not need Jesus in my life began to erode. In fact, I actually wanted what these believers had, and began my own personal quest to discover who their Jesus was.

Don and I continued to attend their meetings and also began reading books by contemporary Christian authors. Don devoured the books. Eventually, Don recommitted himself to Christ in a new and deeper way.

What followed was very unsettling for me. Don was different. He spent his free time reading the Bible. I felt like there was a growing chasm between us. He was so focused on spiritual matters that I was jealous. Who was this Jesus that He could have such a profound effect on my husband? The more I met with our friends the more I realized it was time to resolve my issues with Jesus.

As I opened up about my need for Christ, I came to understand that He was so much more than a "good rabbi" as I had always considered him. It was hard for me to give up my "I am a good person" beliefs and admit my need for a Savior. I had not thought of myself as a sinner, but now I was beginning to see that I was indeed sinful. I had already made peace with God, but was reluctant to acknowledge the divinity and necessity of Jesus. I prayed every day, *God please reveal your Son to me*. One day, I was talking to a friend about God and without any effort on my part, I began sharing about my relationship with His Son, Jesus.

My prayer was answered. No bells, no whistles, or a specific time I can determine. Through my willing heart and the work of the Holy Spirit, God slowly revealed His Son to me in a quiet and personal way.

Don and I were changed by our deepening faith in Jesus Christ. Our marriage was strengthened as we were united in purpose, studying God's word and praying each day for His guidance. Daily I was learning more about myself, and the challenging act of surrendering my will to God's will.

In 1972 Pat, Gordon, Don and I had the opportunity to travel together to the Holy Land. It was an amazing experience to walk where the men and women of the Bible had trod.

When our tour guide first mentioned the opportunity to be rededicated in the Jordan River, where John the Baptist had baptized Jesus, I was skeptical. It sounded too touristy for me. I did not think I needed to participate, however, I could not deny the feeling that God was urging me to make this public declaration of faith. I was reluctant, but when Don and the others expressed an interest, I agreed.

When our tour bus arrived at the riverbank, the casual and almost festive atmosphere of those already milling around surprised me. I had expected this to be a solemn event, with inspirational singing and the reading of scripture. Instead, it appeared that there was no official ceremony, just tourists taking turns entering the waters and wading out to the pastors. Those on the riverbank continued to talk and laugh distractedly, taking little notice of the activity in the water.

Offended by the lack of reverence, I hung back, hesitant to even participate. *God, how can you be honored in the midst of this chaos?* I questioned. I was the last of our group to finally enter the frigid waters. It was December and it had even snowed earlier on our tour.

God, how can you be honored in the midst of this chaos?

Each time I was submerged I came up gasping for air, only to be plunged back down again. I was fighting for my breath when I finally

71

climbed out of the river and made my way to the bus. It was then that I realized I had delayed the whole group.

I had come prepared with a change of clothing, but it was difficult to undress discreetly on the bus while everyone waited outside. I peeled the wet clothing from my shivering body. I was cold, irritated and miserable after such a disappointing experience, so different from what I had hoped. I wanted to cry and longed to climb into a cozy warm bed, forgetting the whole ordeal, but I could not.

The next day I took my seat on the tour bus, asking God, *what was that three ring circus about anyway? I was obedient to you, but it felt all wrong.* As I was deep in thought, a woman boarded the bus and slipped onto the seat next to me. She leaned over and surprised me by saying, "I want to tell you how blessed I was when I saw what looked like a glow surround you each time you were immersed in the water." I was perplexed and told her, "You have the wrong person, it *definitely* was not me." She then described the shirt I had been wearing. It was me. She quietly left the seat, leaving me to consider her words.

I slowly realized the answer to my question. What was it all about? It was all about God, but I had been so caught up in myself, that I had missed Him. The setting was not "all wrong." It was my heart that was wrong. God planned a celebration, hoping I would join in on the joy of those on the riverbank, but I had remained rigid, unable to see that He can be anywhere and in any setting.

Gordon experienced the joy of the moment. He shared with me that he was one of the first to enter the water, rushing forward to rededicate his life to the Lord. As the pastor prepared to dunk him, he eagerly threw himself back into the same frigid waters. He rejoiced in the special opportunity to declare his love for his Savior.

Don shared with me that it had been a special and meaningful moment for him when he stood on the riverbank, imagining that special day when God spoke from heaven, declaring the divinity of Christ. He was confused by my reaction and sad that I had missed the joy God intended.

This was a powerful lesson. God was clearly teaching me to give up my desire for control. He longed for me to see beyond my circumstances and to be ready to receive His blessings, even when they manifested themselves in unexpected places—like a chaotic riverbank.

I returned home, ready to surrender and follow wherever Christ led. I not only understood my own need for a Savior, Jesus Christ, but also God's almighty ability to be present and working in all settings. Little did I know that in His infinite wisdom these experiences were equipping and preparing me to humbly travel the world, where I could proclaim the truth of Jesus Christ and readily receive His blessings, no matter how unusual the circumstances.

10

Eyeglasses, Lord?

"I wish you could have seen the look on their faces! How they laughed or cried for joy when their world came into focus." Betty's face nearly glowed as she recalled her experiences. She and her husband Gary, our oral surgeon from the first medical team, had just returned from their own personal trip to Haiti where they were invited to serve at Gladys and Roland's newly established Togetherness in Christ Medical Clinic.

With no medical training Betty had wondered what she would do in Haiti. A series of circumstances led her to bring several brown paper bags filled with used eyeglasses. She separated the eyeglasses into two categories; one was for weaker strengths, the other for stronger. Her testing tool was a traditional eye chart. Sadly, she found that many Haitians needed to search through the brown bag with the stronger prescriptions.

"Once they had the proper strength glasses on, many of the elderly turned to their grandchildren, joyfully studying their faces." Betty's voice wavered as a wave of emotion washed over her. "I nearly cried when I realized that, if their vision had blurred before the child was born, they might be seeing that child's features in detail for the first time!"

Her enthusiasm was contagious as she shared her many stories of men and women tearfully thanking her with hugs. Some even stated that with the improved vision, they could return to work.

"I had not realized the importance of the eyeglasses until I witnessed their reactions." Betty stated, "I only wished I had brought more."

Don and I listened with intense interest.

Eyeglasses, Lord? I thought. It was a simple process and seemed profoundly successful.

Don and I prayed and asked God, *is this a new ministry that we could offer?* We began exploring what it would take to bring eyeglasses to Haiti. After our experience on the medical teams, we knew that there was the potential for hundreds of people to attend and benefit from an eyeglass clinic. It was exciting to think that we might have the means to help improve the Haitians' sight.

Both of us had poor vision; we understood how difficult it would be to go through the day without our glasses. We knew that for some, improved sight could mean the ability to return to a job or skill, allowing them to provide once again for their family.

We considered the details of how to carry out an eyeglass clinic and felt that we could develop a system similar to our medical clinics. We could set up various testing stations for the individual to pass through. Don was passionate about this possible new ministry. He spent hours contacting optometrists. We asked questions: "How do you perform an eye test with a language barrier or for those who are illiterate and cannot name the letters? What is the best and most accurate way to determine the correct strength?"

For an eye chart we were introduced to a universal chart that used pictures of hands in different positions—fingers facing up, down or to either side. Those tested would mimic with their own hands the picture that the tester pointed to.

For accurate testing we were advised to use special "flipper lenses" with different strengths. Each flipper had two sets of prescription lenses attached and a handle for the tester. The tester would hold the flippers up to the individuals face as though they were eyeglasses for them to look through. Then flip them over and test the second prescription option, asking which was better. A tester might need to go through several sets of flipper lenses with different strengths to finally find the right one.

Don and many others worked diligently to develop this new concept of an eyeglass clinic. Once we felt confident that we could run one, we put the word out about the need for used eyeglasses. Many churches began collecting. An optician assisted us in the reading and organizing of the used glasses, using a lensometer to read the strength of the lens and to determine if they were for near or farsighted correction. It was also helpful to determine if there was a correction for astigmatism. We learned that eyeglasses with high astigmatism correction would, over time, produce a headache and should not be dispensed.

Our heads were spinning with the new knowledge and with the excitement of providing improved vision for the Haitians. In just a year's time from our first departure to Haiti, I had returned three times and was now seriously exploring the idea of returning to provide used eyeglasses.

As I sat once again to journal, staring out our front window at the newly budding spring leaves, I had an overwhelming sense that God was calling Don and me to this new ministry which was only beginning to bud.

Although exhilarated, I was also concerned about how to go forward. I worried about becoming that "well intentioned naive Christian" who did more harm overseas than good.

I prayed and sought wisdom from the Lord. Then I learned about a week-long medical missionary conference that was to be held in Georgia. Rejoicing, I knew that God was leading me, showing me that he had plans to train me. I did not have to figure this out on my own. *Lord, again you are right there, answering my prayers almost before I can say them!*

...*"well intentioned naive Christian" who did more harm overseas than good.*

❖ ❖ ❖

I left for Georgia, eager to soak in all that the conference offered, but God, in His goodness, knew that I needed more than just a deeper understanding of missions. He knew that I needed to experience Him.

Early on the first morning I noticed a small empty chapel tucked away on the campus. I stepped inside, taking in the peaceful interior. A beautifully created stained glass window caught my attention. This low-lying window depicted the traditional picture of Jesus Christ as he knelt and prayed the night before His death.

I found myself drawn to the image and without really thinking, knelt beside the stained glass portrayal of Jesus, resting my shoulder on the cool glass. I felt as though I was leaning into Jesus, wanting to get as close to Him as physically possible. The sun streamed through the window, bathing us in its brilliance. In that moment His presence filled my soul; it was as though He was reaching out to touch me as I was leaning in to touch Him. Peace filled my soul as I sat with Jesus.

Eventually, I left the solitude of the tiny chapel to become one of the thousand medical missionaries gathered from the four corners of the earth. I was probably one of the few non-medical attendees, but my three short-term teams to Haiti gave me a brief insight into the challenges of medicine and foreign ministry. The seminars focused on evangelism through medicine, healing the body and ministering to the spirit. I could relate through my own experiences of the doors our medical teams had opened for our hosts to share their faith.

I grew in my understanding and respect for other cultures. One lecture challenged my traditional North American-centric thinking when they presented world maps with other nations in the center. I found looking at these maps disorienting and realized I had never considered how other nations see the world. Of course their maps would look different! My understanding continued to be challenged as I learned that what was typically called the "third world" was actually the "two-thirds world" in landmass and population.

In one of the most influential lectures, an experienced missionary shared his wisdom about working successfully in missions through an example he called the Second Fiddle Model. He gave this simple illustration, helping us visualize the role of the missionary: "The missionary is to be the second fiddle, *the national always plays first violin.*" This visual helped me see how important it is that our visiting short-term mission teams be there to support the nationals' work. I was overwhelmed with the

> "The missionary is to be the second fiddle, the national always plays first violin."

thought that I did not want to bring teams that would usurp the beauty of the first violin, our host, by being a loud overbearing second fiddle. I just wanted to play my part well in God's symphony. As the lectures continued, it became clear to me that to play my part well, I had a lot to learn about God's perspective on His beloved people around the world.

My notebook was filling up with the wisdom of these missionaries. They made a deep imprint on me. I was exchanging my prejudices and pre-conceived impressions for their truths gained from decades of foreign ministry.

I had come to the conference with certain concerns regarding our new ministry. One of those was the ability to accurately communicate to new team members the importance of being spiritually prepared for their mission experience. I felt inadequate in my ability to guide them. On the last day of the conference, God answered my prayer through a conversation with a missionary who told me about the Servanthood Bible Study. This Bible study on serving, created by his ministry, was perfect for us! He encouraged me to reproduce it for our teams. I could now rely on the wisdom of others, who had thoroughly explored the topic of servanthood, to guide our future team members, keeping the focus on God and not on our good works.

My head and heart were wrapped around the sessions, demanding all my concentration. The highlight of each day was the early morning appointment I kept with Jesus. I could abandon all my concerns and simply bask in His presence in the little chapel set apart from all the hustle and bustle. Every morning He was there in His sunlit glory, inviting me to approach Him and kneel, leaning into Him as we had those intimate moments together, basking in silence. Through my time spent in prayer and the learning I gained in the sessions, my anxiety about being the naïve Christian was replaced with an inner peace and confidence. Yes, I was naïve, but I knew that God was guiding and training me.

After a week of early mornings with Jesus and seminars that thrust me into a new worldview, I returned home energized and committed to apply all I learned and experienced to my future efforts in ministry. I realized how little I knew about missions and found myself longing for more knowledge, eagerly enrolling in correspondence courses from the Billy Graham Institute. I devoured all the recommended readings; it was fuel for my passion. Holding on to the "Second Fiddle" illustration my deep desire now was to learn how to do missions from God's perspective and to be a blessing to our foreign hosts.

As I sat journaling my thoughts of the conference, I treasured my memories of the time spent in prayer and how refreshing it was. The Lord knew I needed that precious time with Him, to be quiet in the midst of such incredible activity, not just the commotion of the conference, but the activity of my life. Running my full-time daycare, while being consumed with thoughts of Haiti and the details of organizing trips, was taking a toll. I was energized by the teams to Haiti, but the pace at which it was all happening was overwhelming. It was good to spend the time in quiet prayer, renewing my heart and spirit.

I returned home to prepare for yet another adventure—our first Haitian eyeglass clinic.

11

Seeing Clearly

I heard a scream, then shouts. "No!" "Stop!"

The sounds came from inside our first Haitian eyeglass clinic. Sheets, hung as walls, prevented me from seeing the cause of the commotion. I left my post to investigate. When I arrived, I found our distribution station in disarray. Eyeglasses, typically displayed neatly on tables, were scattered on the ground.

A young Haitian man had burst through the back "wall"—a divider sheet—startling everyone as he grabbed as many of the glasses as he could. Of course, now he was nowhere to be seen.

It was February of 1991 and we were back in Haiti, exactly one year after our medical team to the island of La Gonave. This was the debut of our new temporary eyeglass clinic, set up to serve the people of Cite Soleil. Our clinic was on the outskirts of the city, on open and barren land, avoiding the tightly packed huts.

Local pastor Rev. Louis had recently purchased this large piece of property and was in the process of building a school on it. The newly-laid cement foundation was the site for our clinic. There were no walls built yet, just tall re-rod bars sticking out of the foundation. We attached our sheets and canopies to these, creating the several stations needed for testing, distributing and fitting of eyeglasses.

The clinic had been running smoothly, but we did not realize the value of our well-stocked inventory. For many Haitians the cost of one pair of glasses was equivalent to a full year's wage. Our display was an irresistible temptation! We moved the table away from the temporary wall, hoping to discourage any future thieves.

We also provided medical care on this team with several nurses who were seeing patients in an enclosed tent to provide privacy during examination. How fortunate that this enclosure protected the medicines from thieves. Although the tent felt like a sauna inside, they were able to help hundreds of patients without any incidents.

When we arrived that morning, several hundred Haitians were waiting. I wasn't surprised. There was a great need for eyeglasses. We came prepared with numbered tickets, hoping to keep the crowds under control. It was my job to call out the numbers, which I had learned in Creole, their native language. I then led the ticket holder to a bench near our first testing station. There they waited, observing the person ahead of them being tested. This prepared them for their own experience.

I enjoyed my position which allowed me to watch the Haitians' expressions as the testers rotated the flippers from the lesser to the stronger strengths. Often those who needed the stronger strengths would become excited, pointing to the face of the tester or the surrounding area. They smiled and laughed as their world came into focus. For many, it was a life-changing experience.

For our youngest son David, a senior in high school, this was his first trip to Haiti. He worked as one of the testers. I loved watching how meticulously he helped the Haitians find their correct prescription strength. Don and I were delighted to finally introduce David to the people and culture that meant so much to us.

As we settled back into our stations after the unexpected theft, another problem developed. An industrious group of Haitians were counterfeiting our tickets and selling them. At first, I was very confused by the duplicate numbers. Eventually, the culprits were discovered and stopped, but not before many people had purchased the fake tickets. It broke our hearts when we realized we did not have the time or supplies to serve those with the false tickets.

I was trying to convince the false ticket holders that we could not test them when I realized that my decision would not be accepted in Haitian culture. I was a woman! A man needed to make the final declaration. So, we recruited David who was six foot three inches and seventeen years old, to be the official ticket assessor. In full view of the crowd, he carefully examined the false tickets, making a big show with the appropriate gestures. After examination he would announce that they were no good. That settled it.

Our theft problem, however, was harder to solve. Even with the table moved, desperate Haitians continued to duck under the sheets, frantically grabbing at glasses. Eventually, we hired a guard with a billy club to chase the culprits away. A few men continued to grab at the glasses, but the presence of the guard helped.

As we discussed our theft problem with Rev. Louis, he shared that some Haitians take more than just eyeglasses. The current laws allowed Haitians to legally take land. The law permitted individuals to construct a basic home on any property, then lay claim to that portion—even if someone else owned it.

Rev. Louis feared that the people would invade his land and begin building. Just laying a few blocks for the foundation was enough to claim the land, even if the home was never completed. Once there, the laws would render the pastor powerless to remove them. We were all worried. Later, when Don and I returned to the States, Don wrote a grant that funded a protective wall around Rev. Louis' property.

After solving our duplicate ticket issue and doing our best to discourage the thieves, the rest of our clinic days progressed as expected. We went back to the United States with the satisfaction of providing 670 Haitians with eyeglasses. We were convinced that with some minor changes, we could continue to successfully provide free eyeglasses to more underserved people.

We were eager to spread the word about our work. We sent letters around the world to foreign pastors and missionaries about our new short-term mission ministry of construction teams and medical and eyeglasses clinics. Due to the challenges of international airmail, it took time to receive a response. During this time Don and I continued to organize more teams to Haiti, mostly construction teams.

Eventually, we heard from a missionary in Panama City, Pastor Wetzstein, who was interested in an eyeglass clinic. It was exciting for me to consider a new country and culture. We did our research and in 1993 a team was formed and we were on our way.

Panama City is a large and modern coastal urban area. There were highways, cars, trucks and buses. There were no donkeys with carts. Due to the American presence in Panama City because of the Panama Canal, there were many familiar sights. We even passed *El Hogar del Whopper, Berger King*—The Home of the Whopper, Burger King!

As we traveled, our host surprised us by tossing a gum wrapper out his car window. Our group was indignant. He explained that he was actually doing his duty as a good Panamanian; he was creating work for the street sweepers. Men and women who received welfare were expected to work, picking up the trash. Littering was encouraged!

Pastor Wetzstein's church was a large white stucco building surrounded by stately palm trees and green grass. Unlike Haiti, Panama is rich with vegetation.

The church was situated on a busy thoroughfare in a suburb of Panama City. A veranda connected it to a large office building next door. The team settled into the all-purpose quarters where the team would stay. The space was large enough to sleep, eat and meet together. While the team slept on air mattresses, Don and I were invited to sleep upstairs in the pastor's office, which was also a guest room. Such luxury! Our own space with comfortable beds! It was a stark contrast to our earlier experiences in parts of Haiti.

During our team meeting, Pastor Wetzstein explained the two ministries of his church and the international organization, Christ For All Nations (*Cristo Para Todas Las Naciones*), whose headquarters were housed in this office building. Both ministries actively reached out to the community. Christ For All Nations conducted radio broadcasts and operated a large printing press. They provided wonderful Bible studies and other written materials in Spanish. Pastor Wetzstein was eager to share this literature with those who would visit our clinic.

After we settled into our new lodging, the pastor took us to visit a local Kuna Indian village only thirty minutes outside of the city. As we approached, it felt like we had entered a different world. The Kuna Indians are indigenous Panamanians who still live in traditional ways. Their homes are made with sticks, thatched roofs and mud floors.

In contrast to their bare and earthy living conditions, the women were stunning. They wore brightly colored traditional dresses with beads wrapped around their arms and rings in their noses. Their customary dress, called molas, were fascinating. They consisted of many different colored fabrics intricately stitched together to create beautiful designs. The men wore typical North American styled shirts and pants.

We joined them for an evening Bible study. While the outdoor service was inspiring, the dogs and chickens that roamed around our legs were distracting.

Although we told the village chiefs about our upcoming eyeglass clinic in the city, we knew from locals that they were a shy people. It was a long bus ride from their remote village, and it was unlikely they would come. A local missionary even said they all had good eyesight, since he had never seen any of them wearing glasses. I hoped he was right.

We returned to the city and prepared for our clinic. In an effort to avoid overcrowding, we had asked Pastor Wetzstein to preregister those we would be serving. By assigning individuals a specific day to arrive, we hoped to create a more peaceful experience for everyone. We estimated that we could serve about 100 people each day.

On the first day our new system worked well. What a relief! It was nice to not feel overwhelmed. Our attendees arrived early and gathered under the veranda. This was the perfect time to introduce our new witness tool. We came prepared to tell the salvation story of Jesus using bracelets with colored beads in a specific order on a leather strap. The color of each bead was significant, a good visual of our sin, Christ's sacrifice, God's forgiveness and the promise of Heaven.

I had hoped to use them in Haiti but was advised against it. The bracelets were too similar to the fetishes and charms used in voodoo worship. To give them a bracelet could inadvertently encourage syncretism, the blending of worship of Christ with the worship of evil spirits. We did not want to confuse the Haitians. They needed to understand Christ alone; there are no fetishes or objects needed for faith.

Here in Panama, we were encouraged to use the bracelets, preassembled by ministry volunteers. We knew the great potential of this simple visual aid. Through an interpreter team members explained the deeper meaning of the bracelets' colors. We were able to witness to all the adults and children, placing a bracelet on their arm and giving them a written explanation in Spanish with related scriptures.

As our day progressed, we were pleasantly surprised by a visit from four of the Kuna village chiefs, who braved the bus ride into the city. They arrived with a newspaper. Their desire was simple, to read the news. I found it odd to think of these men reading about current world events. I had equated their simple lifestyle with illiteracy and a detachment from modern civilization. I was wrong. With the paper as our testing tool, we made sure that each one was satisfied with their new glasses. Each left with a smile on his face while holding their new reading glasses.

On Tuesday morning when we arrived at the clinic, we were not prepared for what we saw. Eighty Kuna Indians were waiting for us! The women stood out in their bright traditional dress. The four chiefs, pleased with their new glasses, had returned with the adults from their village. We were thrilled to see them, but questioned our ability to serve everyone. So much for our efforts at solving the overcrowding problem!

The team was determined to serve all those Kuna Indians even if it meant pushing themselves to the point of exhaustion. We loved the fact that the women arrived with their fabric, needle and thread to make sure that with their new glasses they could see the tiny stitches required to create their molas. We knew that selling the molas to tourists was an important part of the Kuna economy. We learned that the local missionary was wrong; each one of the Kuna Indians we tested did need glasses.

The following morning Don and I discussed the addition of the Kuna Indians. While we were excited to serve this tribe, it created more uncertainty and stress. In our discussions Don and I realized that he preferred more organized, predictable situations; I enjoyed the problem solving that comes with uncertainty. This was a revelation. Originally, when the ministry began, we assumed that we would both lead teams. But we had been naïve. We had not taken into account that we were different individuals, with our own unique skills to offer to the ministry. Through our discussions and prayers, we felt God leading us to the conclusion that I would continue to lead teams while Don would focus on developing the eyeglass ministry and continue his responsibilities of bookkeeper and grant writer.

With our roles redefined, both Don and I returned home from Panama with renewed commitment, confident that we were right where God wanted us. Don felt especially passionate regarding the eyeglass ministry and worked diligently to help it grow.

As word spread, we received an increasing amount of glasses. Eventually, the opticians who volunteered their time and equipment to read and sort the glasses could not keep up. We realized we needed our own equipment.

Through Don's efforts we received a grant allowing us to purchase three used lensometers. Several women agreed to be trained on the equipment, which they kept in their homes. This allowed them to wash, read and label the glasses at their convenience.

Even with the increase in donations, we still needed more glasses. With each team potentially distributing over 500 pairs of glasses, Don knew we would need several thousand pairs in our inventory. He contacted a representative of the Lions Club, an organization dedicated to recycling used eyeglasses, with collection sites nationwide. The Indiana representative agreed to provide our ministry with a steady supply, if Don would drive there and pick them up, which he did. Many of the eyeglasses were even presorted and labeled by prisoners through a state program.

It was clear that God was guiding the eyeglass ministry. The energy and enthusiasm were contagious. Our pastor offered extra storage space in his basement for the boxes. A videographer helped create an eyeglass team training video, free of charge. Volunteers were always available and eager to help. We had momentum! It was exciting!

12

Looking for a Millionaire

Moving forward sometimes means looking backward. As Don and I gained momentum with the ministry, we began to wonder if it was time for me to consider retiring from my in-home daycare business to run the ministry full-time. As I considered this change, I found myself remembering times that our ventures didn't work out so well. It made me more cautious about giving up financial security again. Plus, Don and I were no spring chickens. Should we really be starting something new at our age?

I also felt self-doubt because of my gender. I grew up in an era when women were not leaders, but it was now the 1990's. Women had fought for rights while proving themselves in the workplace. The culture had changed. It was now possible for me to be a director of a global ministry. I wished I could slip back in time to encourage my younger self, who feared at one time that her life would be restricted by being a girl. I would have told her that exciting days of great adventures were yet to come!

I also wished I could speak to the committee that decided that, as a married woman, I no longer needed my scholarship and education. My first twenty-five years out of school might have looked like failure, staying home raising kids, never working within my field. Yet here I was, creating a ministry based on sociological principles, understanding and assessing group dynamics and exploring how cultures interact. My degree, which I fought so hard for, created a solid foundation for the ministry.

What about our age? Was I really considering beginning something new at fifty-six? And Don at fifty-eight? That sounded so old! We did not feel old; in fact, we felt energized and excited. Don and I had the time and energy to invest in this ministry. Although we were beginning the empty nest phase of life, we did not feel empty because we had a purpose and a passion.

All of our concerns and fears didn't keep me or Don from moving forward in our new roles. While Don was busy collecting and sorting eyeglasses, I continued to organize and lead teams. Gladys and Roland, the Haitian couple who served with us on our medical clinics, asked if we could provide several construction teams. They also asked if we could provide instruction for women in the trade of basket weaving. Although I had no basket weaving skills, I soon found women who did. We set a date. I also formed teams to serve a local ministry, the Detroit Rescue Mission, where we constructed a playground and performed other needed tasks. I tackled all of this while still operating my in-home daycare.

The team serving Detroit was created in response to the repeated request by church members for a local and inexpensive short-term mission experience. When we began recruiting for this stateside team, however, no one wanted to participate. In fact, some of the very same people who had requested working on a local team ended up joining our Haiti teams! Don and I found ourselves scrambling at the last minute, relying on friends to help us with the commitment to build the playground. With little interest by team members for local teams we felt that God's calling on the ministry was to focus on international service opportunities.

I enjoyed juggling multiple teams, all at different stages of preparation. As a team would form, I made it a priority to meet several times. With each new team, my confidence grew in how to prepare and lead. Training manuals were developed specific to each country and mission. I even created a re-entry manual to help team members process their experiences when they returned. It was wonderful to see how God would speak to each team member, revealing Himself in new ways as they served.

With no computers or Internet, the manuals were time-consuming to develop. I spent hours in the library researching cultural information. When I located a relevant article, I copied it, and then did the original version of "cutting and pasting" … with scissors and tape!

Eventually, I was overwhelmed. I averaged leading three teams a year and still worked full-time. It was too much. Don and I were ready for me to close my daycare and focus on the ministry. However, we knew we did not have the resources to cover the loss of my income and still pay our bills, and we certainly could not continue paying the large expenses for foreign travel required with each team.

To cover our financial needs I began to hope and pray that God would move within the heart of someone with great wealth—a millionaire—to be so inspired by the good that we were doing that they would commit to financially supporting our ministry. *Lord,* I prayed, *You have clearly shown that this ministry is Yours. Please provide for our needs.* In my heart I thought I knew how He should provide and was waiting for that exciting day when we would meet our wealthy benefactor.

As only God can orchestrate, I came across a magazine article titled, "Are You Waiting for That Millionaire So You Can Do Missions?" I scoured the article, but the message of the author was not a how-to plan. It was a message of a very different sort. The author reminded the reader that it is often *not* God's plan to provide everything we need ahead of time, but to provide for our needs as they arise, causing us to rely on Him. God knows that if we have all we need, it is our human nature to run ahead, depending less on Him and more on ourselves. That burst my bubble! Perhaps there would be no millionaire; perhaps God wanted us to be dependent on Him.

Although my heart agreed with the article, my mind wrestled with putting so much trust in God over finances. This short-term mission ministry was not the first time that Don and I felt called to serve God full-time. Several years ago we owned a Christian bookstore, but right after we opened our doors, the economy took a turn for the worse.

> Perhaps there would be no millionaire; perhaps God wanted us to be dependent on Him.

It was 1974 and our prayer group had been enthusiastic about Don's desire to open the store. They saw it as a way for the group to reach out to the community. They even committed to volunteer their time. The location, just blocks from a state university, seemed perfect. Don, cautious about such a venture, sought the counsel of many successful local business owners. They all agreed that this was a wise investment, and as Christians, they agreed it would provide a needed ministry to the community. They even agreed to contribute to the financial base of developing the business. They purchased the inventory, paid for needed renovations, and covered other start-up costs. With their financial commitment and much prayer we all felt confident that God was leading us to open this bookstore.

In December of 1974 Logos Bookstore of Ypsilanti, Michigan opened its doors. At this time the surrounding businesses were thriving. Shortly after our grand opening, however, the nation went into a deep recession. We watched as longtime merchants on the block closed their doors. As the buildings became vacant, the new tenants were appealing to a different clientele. The drugstore became a liquor store and the clothing store became a billiards and game room. These customers were not interested in Christian books.

Those were difficult and lean years. During this time our prayer group committed to provide for our family. They generously opened a bank account for us and filled it with their personal donations. This allowed us to pay our bills, guaranteeing our family's security. Though it was challenging to accept money from friends, I was incredibly grateful, knowing that their generosity kept us from losing our home and put food on the table. That taught me to graciously accept help from others and to see the love of Christ through their actions.

After several years Don made the decision to step down as manager. The bookstore continued under new management, but never recovered. Eventually the doors were closed and the inventory sold. The members of the board of directors, many of them friends, paid all the bills from their own personal finances. Because of their generosity we avoided bankruptcy, however, those who invested in the store lost their entire investment.

Don was able to return to work in his field of educational research and we slowly recovered from our financial losses. The bookstore was a very difficult chapter in our married life, leaving painful wounds as we searched for the meaning behind our struggles. Although confused and frustrated, we were still confident it had been God's will. We knew it had served the community and been a blessing to those who shopped there. Why God did not intervene during the economic downturn, we didn't understand. It was at this time, with our finances depleted, that I began my home daycare business.

Although confused and frustrated, we were still confident that it had been God's will.

❖ ❖ ❖

Thirteen years later I read the message of the article and reluctantly let go of my dream of a millionaire. I was flooded with emotions as I remembered our past struggles and feared returning to those desperate conditions.

It had been difficult for me to accept the help of our friends. I was incredibly grateful, yet struggled with the feelings of dependence on others. As I considered going forward with no wealthy benefactor I found it just as hard to depend on God as it was to depend on others.

Thankfully, through prayer, God showed me that this situation was different. With the bookstore we had entered the ministry assuming that it could provide for us. This time Don would continue in his full-time position, guaranteeing an income. We could also prepare and find financial support before I left my business. As I considered all of this, God spoke to my heart with two simple words, *Trust Me*.

It was difficult at first, but when our church mission committee agreed to help support us, I was encouraged. That gave me the courage to also ask our family and closest friends. They agreed. With the commitment for financial support in place, I retired from my home daycare business.

Our dependence on others reminded me that this ministry was not ours, but God's ministry. It existed, not because of our great organizational or leadership skills, but because God was moving in the hearts of so many. Just as we were dependent on others for our finances, we were also dependent on all of those who volunteered. Each person was an integral and needed part of the ministry, from the team members to those who served by preparing eyeglasses or sorting medicines.

In January of 1993, to honor the commitments from donors, we began the official process of applying for a non-profit tax exemption. Don and I filled out the needed forms together, line by line.

Then we read a question that caused us to stop abruptly, pen in hand. It asked, "What is the name of the organization?" Looking at one another, we realized that we had never given our ministry a name. *A name,* I thought, *oh Lord, there is so much in a name!*

I felt the weight of the task as I stared at a blank sheet of paper, hoping for some inspiration. Hours were spent, scribbling ideas, and then crossing them out. It seemed hopeless. Finally, after much effort and prayer, the name Mission Opportunities Short Term emerged from all of the false starts. *Yes, Lord, that is exactly who we are—Mission Opportunities Short Term, abbreviated nicely to MOST Ministries.* It was with great joy that I filled in the empty space with our newfound name.

> Yes, Lord, that is exactly who we are—Mission Opportunities Short Term...

The detailed form also required a list of names for a board of directors to oversee the ministry. Several friends committed to this important role.

The maturing of the ministry thrilled us. Don and I eagerly anticipated the many ways that God would use Mission Opportunities Short Term. In just a few months we would be leaving with an eyeglass team to Latvia. We did not know what this new country would be like or how God would use MOST Ministries, but we were ready and willing to follow where God was leading and I was at peace. We did not need a millionaire; we needed to keep our eyes on Christ and trust Him.

13

A Ray of Light Pierces the Darkness

This place is seething with lies! That was all I could think as I stood in the doorway. A mountain of old communist propaganda books and pamphlets, waist deep, filled the room. It was the fall of 1993 and Don and I were in Riga, Latvia, standing in the old Communist Propaganda and Training Facility—the heart of the lies.

I felt disgust at the sight of these written works, knowing they were filled with manipulative words telling the starving and deprived Latvians how lucky they had been to be living under the Soviet's communist regime. The truth was that many under communism experienced severe poverty and deprivation. People stood in long lines for hours just for a loaf of bread or a pair of shoes.

The Latvians were now free from this oppressive regime. They had achieved independence in 1991, just two years earlier. During their recovery the local church provided the new government with documentation showing they had once owned this building. It was returned to them. The church members worked hard to remove the offensive propaganda that had been left behind, dumping it in this small room as they cleared the rest of the building. Soon, a truck would arrive to remove and destroy all of the material.

I was grateful when our host moved on, showing us the clean and open rooms of this three-hundred-year-old stone building. Our hosts had recently transformed the building into the new Christian Medical and Family Center. This was to be our lodging and site for our upcoming temporary eyeglass clinic.

Our eyeglass team was to be their first outreach into the community. They hoped to attract people to the clinic who might then return for future medical services. They also wanted to create a permanent eyeglass clinic at this site, inspired by our temporary clinics. We loved the idea and worked hard to locate a European organization that could provide their clinic with a steady supply of used eyeglasses. We were eager to teach them our techniques.

On September 13, 1993 Don and I, along with eighteen team members, landed in the European-style capital city of Riga, Latvia. It is the largest city in the Baltic States, and has an active port. We passed over old bridges, surrounded by churches with tall spires and courtyards with elegant statues, which displayed the rich history of this city and its people. The cobblestoned streets of historic Old Town were lined with buildings from centuries past, each with decorative and colorful facades.

Many women wore traditional Russian babushkas, a scarf covering their hair and tied under their chin as protection against the chilly autumn air. I wondered how many of these women were actually from Russia.

In the 1940's when the Soviet Union's proverbial "Iron Curtain" closed off Eastern Europe, over 50,000 Latvians were arrested and shipped to distant regions within the Soviet Union, some to Siberian concentration and labor camps. Stalin heartlessly uprooted individuals and separated families, moving them as though they were pawns in a chess game. To fill the void he strategically enticed Russians to immigrate into the newly occupied Baltic States, with easy access to jobs and apartments. Latvia became a mix of Russians and Latvians.

After its independence many Russians remained in Latvia. Some had lived in the region for fifty years, while others were born there; this was their home. These individuals were now forced to adjust to this newly-freed country, no longer under Russian rule which had provided them with jobs and a sense of security.

On our way to our lodging we passed the pride of the city: the elegant Latvian Freedom Monument, comparable to our Statue of Liberty. Built in 1935, the statue honors those who fought for freedom from the Russian Empire in the early 1900's. The statue consists of a tall column topped with a graceful copper woman draped in a robe, holding three gold stars above her head. I was surprised that during their occupation the Soviets had not destroyed this inspiring monument. Instead, they had attempted to rewrite the history, stating that it was a statue to honor Mother Russia. To the Latvians it always represented their hope for freedom.

It was at the base of this monument in 1987 that 5,000 Latvians took the risk to gather and lay flowers in honor of the tens of thousands of individuals who had been sent to Siberian labor camps. The Latvians were still under Russian rule, but they sensed that the grip of the Soviet Union was weakening.

Not far from our lodging was another statue, the Riflemen Monument. It was built by the Soviets. It was not elegant, just big and threatening. Three tall stone soldiers in trench coats stood shoulder to shoulder, facing outwards, on a large stone base. No matter from where you viewed it, you were always under one of the soldier's menacing and watchful eyes. It was an unsettling feeling. I wondered if the freed Latvians would remove this fear-inducing statue, or leave it as a reminder of their recent past.

Dr. Vilnis Sosars, one of the Latvian Christian doctors who had invited our MOST Ministries' team to this country, welcomed us. After our tour of the building we settled into our quarters on the third floor. We regrouped in the main clinic room on the first floor to discuss the upcoming eyeglass clinic. The Latvian doctors, nurses and volunteers were eager to begin their training.

After we described our testing process we asked about the needs of those we would be serving. Our hosts shared their deep concern regarding their countrymen's need to learn about Christ and the basics of Christianity.

During the Russian occupation the atheistic Communist Party silenced all Christians. It was illegal to practice or speak of one's faith and the penalty was imprisonment or even worse, being sent to a Siberian labor or concentration camp. All churches were closed and Bibles destroyed. Priests were arrested and sent to camps.

As a result, generations of Latvians were raised without the knowledge of Christ's love. I wondered what it had been like to be silenced and to live in such fear. Even a strong Christian would be tempted to question the existence of a loving God under such trying circumstances. I admired these Latvians who had clung to their faith despite such hardships.

The doctors and nurses expressed their excitement and joy at being able to finally share the Gospel with the members of their local community. They rejoiced in their new freedom, a freedom I took for granted.

The Latvian clinic staff and volunteers were compassionate and kind, not resentful because of their past hardships as I might have expected. They were optimistic about the future. It was, however, impossible for our team to overlook the sad effects of Latvia's past, as the people bore the emotional and physical scars.

A day before we officially began our eyeglass clinic, we served our first clients: two priests who were nearly blind after spending many years in Siberian concentration camps. They had been sent there because of their faith. One had spent five years in the camp, the other ten. They survived, but the beatings they received and the physical deprivation took a toll on their health, damaging their eyes.

Our optometrist performed many tests and examinations using the special equipment we brought, but, in the end, it was with a heavy heart that he finally informed them that there were no corrections available. The damage was too severe. As I considered the suffering these men had endured, I began to wonder if our team was emotionally prepared for the stories and pain we were about to witness during our clinic. The evidence of hardship and horror was difficult to comprehend. Unfortunately, this was just the first of many sad tales of the past.

The next day a woman and her teenage daughter arrived, both nearly blind. Through the help of an interpreter we listened with disbelief as they shared their story. Ten years earlier, the KGB (Soviet military police) had caught her husband smuggling people out of Latvia and into Sweden. As retribution the KGB came to their home, kicking and beating her and her daughter, who was only four years old at the time, into a state of near blindness.

How could the KGB be so heartless? They seemed like monsters! Yet, did these men not operate out of fear, also? Were they afraid that if they had not carried out their orders, someone would show up at their homes, kicking and beating their families?

As a result of the beatings, the mother and daughter had very poor vision. Again, there were no glasses strong enough to help. In one last desperate attempt to aid the mother, one of our team members offered his lighted magnifying glass.

She placed the magnifier over the page of scripture we were using to test. Her face brightened. "I can read the words!" She exclaimed. "I can read the truth of this Scripture and Jesus! And now I can share it with my daughter." After carefully reading the page, she handed the magnifying glass back to the interpreter. She smiled and thanked him.

I told the interpreter to return it to her and inform her that she could keep it as a gift. She read the page again and again. In a few minutes she returned the magnifying glass to the interpreter. This happened two more times. I wondered why she didn't want to keep it.

I asked the interpreter to make it very clear that this was a gift for her. When she finally understood, she was so shocked that she bolted from her chair, stopping at the nearest window. She held onto the ledge to steady herself as she wept uncontrollably. I was stunned. Was kindness so out of the ordinary in her life experience that it was too much for her to comprehend? *Oh God, what have these people endured!?!* Sadly, the daughter's vision could not be improved.

After they were tested, the mother and daughter were invited to visit our witness station, a room set aside for nationals and team members to share their faith and to offer prayer. A booklet, *"How to Know God,"* was provided in both Russian and Latvian. Herta, our Latvian American team member, was delighted to share her faith in her native language. She sat with the mother and daughter and explained the Scripture booklet. With the help of the magnifying glass the mother read portions herself. She was delighted to have forty-eight pages of scriptures, with explanations, to take home and read to her daughter.

We also gave each of them a witness bracelet. Although the mother and daughter could not see clearly, they could feel and finger the beads as Herta explained their meanings. The daughter, a shy teenager, seemed to enjoy the blurred bright colors and smooth surface of the beads as Herta placed it on her wrist.

In the same room was the Russian interpreter, along with Pastor Mike, our team member, who explained the booklet and witness bracelets to the Russians. Stepping into that room was like being at an international prayer meeting. Russian, Latvian and English prayers filled the air. There were many sad stories told to us by the Russians. They felt displaced and worried for their future. They often asked for prayer, even though they were skeptical of religion.

Another woman at the eyeglass clinic shared with a team member that she was filled with thanksgiving for Americans. When her daughter was young, she received a much-needed blanket and food from the United States. Now she was receiving free glasses. She kept repeating, "I am twice blessed, I am twice blessed."

As I began to understand the depths of the suffering of these people, it caused me to realize the profound effects of the care packages and faithful funds we send from our homes to other countries. They are important and life changing.

I was grateful that Pastor Mike was there to explain that it is the love of Christ that motivates and inspires many of us to reach out and help. I hoped and prayed that they would receive the ultimate blessing, to know Christ as their Savior. I was grateful that God had called us to be in this mission field. We were meeting needs and offering hope. I also considered the many individuals back home who had contributed to allow this blessing, the many MOST Ministries donors and volunteers.

As we worked with our clients, a woman came bounding down the stairs from the second floor, shouting joyfully for all to hear. We asked the interpreter what she was shouting. He translated, "I think I have died and gone to heaven! I have two pair of glasses, one for distance and one for reading." It was wonderful to hear and see their joy as we provided the free eyeglasses and received their grateful hugs.

Don had worked hard over the years to establish an effective and efficient process to move individuals smoothly through our eyeglass clinics. The optometrist, who had been testing patients with his special equipment, decided our system of using the special hand held flippers with different strengths as testing tools, was working so well he would not take the extra time to use his equipment. It was a wonderful endorsement of our process.

Our interpreters, we learned, had barely enough food to eat. We invited them to join us for meals, and while initially they were hesitant, after much encouragement they did so.

One of the interpreters, seeing the fresh bananas on the table, shared with us that he had recently been able to give his sister a banana for her birthday. Her only gift from him! He was sharing his joy in having been able to provide such a delicious gift, but to our ears it was a shocking example of their deprivation. His anecdote spoke volumes to the team members about the lives of these young men and women and provided even more insight into the lives of those we were serving at the clinic.

Although traveling with the ministry to many different countries had brought me face-to-face with human suffering, there was something different about seeing the effects of the Russian occupation and communism. It was difficult for me to comprehend and process the many atrocities committed against these people.

Gloom seemed to surround everyone as they walked the streets with their head down, intentionally avoiding eye contact. No one offered a friendly greeting. People's clothing was pitifully drab, reflecting their demeanor. It was a sad contrast to the nations of Panama and Haiti where colors were brilliant and smiles for foreigners were common.

As Don and our interpreter were out running an errand, they needed help with directions. Don, hoping for some assistance from one of the locals, approached a woman who was walking in front of them. He reached forward and tapped her on the shoulder to get her attention.

As she felt his touch, her whole body stiffened. She was visibly startled. She turned to look at Don with such fear and horror reflected on her face, that he suddenly realized he had done something terribly wrong.

Our interpreter, Astra, a Latvian citizen who was now living in the United States, quickly explained to the woman they meant her no harm. They just needed directions. Astra then explained to Don that with tens of thousands of Latvians deported and imprisoned during the occupation, the people lived in constant fear that it could happen to them at any time. To be safe it was best to blend into the crowd, never drawing attention to yourself. Before their liberation an unexpected tap on the shoulder could mean you had caught the unwanted attention of a Russian soldier. You might be shipped to prison or Siberia for no good reason. Although Latvia was now a free country, years of conditioning caused by fear and oppression were hard to erase.

Ironically, these Russian soldiers who had caused such fear were now stripped of their power and wealth, joining the ranks of the poor in Latvia. As our hosts shared about the hardships for these soldiers left here in Latvia, unwanted by their mother country, our hearts began to soften towards them.

Men, who had served their country with pride, were now selling off bits and pieces of their uniform for food, even their medals. Don worked with our host to purchase a few items. We hoped that our money would help these Russian soldiers as they began a new, albeit difficult life. Don and I saw our purchases as symbols to remind us, and our four children who would be receiving these as gifts at Christmas, how fleeting worldly fame and power can be.

As I ached for their past, my new Latvian friends continued to look forward. The tenderness and compassion provided by the doctors and staff of the Christian Medical and Family Center were a healing balm for the physical and emotional wounds of the people who entered. The knowledge that this site was preparing to set up a permanent eyeglass clinic provided our team with a ray of hope in an otherwise depressing situation. We left Latvia reassured that these caring doctors and staff were committed to bring light into their dark and gloomy world.

We also returned home rejoicing that God had revealed himself in a powerful way to our optometrist. He announced with conviction that he felt called to change his goal in life from providing physical sight, to offering spiritual insight. He planned to become a priest!

On this trip another team member also made a significant decision. Before the team began I asked Steve, a dear friend and fellow team member, to consider being trained as a team leader. He had firmly said he was not interested. However, by the end of this trip, Steve said he could not deny that God was calling him to assist MOST Ministries in this very important volunteer position. Because of his decision our ministry could begin sending out additional teams, meeting more and more needs around the world.

14

On the Home Front

Growth can be exciting and frightening, all at the same time. After the official naming of the ministry in 1993, the ministry grew as God provided new team leaders. I was overjoyed when our dear friend, Steve, announced that he felt called to serve as a team leader. Not long after Steve's commitment I received a phone call from Eileen, a single woman who had also participated on many teams. She too felt called by God to become a team leader for MOST Ministries.

To complete their training Steve and Eileen accompanied me on our first Guatemala trip in 1994. Our team assisted the Kaqchikel Indians in Santiago Zamora in building a septic tank and drain field, the first such sanitation in the village.

As a result of Steve and Eileen's commitment, MOST Ministries was able to send out six teams in 1995, instead of only three a year. We added Macao and Ghana to our growing list of countries.

In 1996 Eileen felt called to leave her current job to work full-time as an assistant for MOST Ministries. I was shocked, since I had not requested help. She even assured me that she would raise her own support. How could I refuse?

At this time I was working out of our home in an upstairs bedroom. We gave Eileen a space in our basement laundry room, a small nook where we set up a card table, chair, typewriter and cordless phone. I enjoyed Eileen's companionship and we functioned well in our two little offices. We shouted through the laundry chute in the hall when we had quick questions for each other. Together we responded to requests from around the world as the ministry grew.

MOST's eyeglass ministry also continued to grow. The amount of glasses pouring in soon overwhelmed our pastor's basement and our garage. Then a church member who owned retail property offered us his storage space. I remember standing in the empty room, in awe of this unexpected donation. I wondered, *what* are *God's plans for MOST Ministries?* It seemed that it was growing at an incredible rate, beyond what Don and I had expected. I then wondered if we would ever fill such a large space. We did, and very quickly. Soon the shelves were filled with donated medicines, witness materials, suitcases and, of course, boxes of sorted eyeglasses.

In 1996 an offer came to rent a suite of rooms on Concordia College's campus, just fifteen minutes from our home. Because of our past experience with the Christian bookstore, Don and I were very cautious with the ministry's finances. We were concerned that the sudden interest in short-term missions might be a fad, but after experiencing several successful years with continued momentum, we felt confident that short-term missions would continue. We signed the lease.

Eileen and I packed up our files, typewriter, card table, chairs, and the new copy and fax machine. I loved the fax machine! Before we owned one, it was difficult to make contact with nationals in foreign countries. Personal computers were expensive and neither our ministry nor our various hosts owned them. International phone calls were challenging with loud static and voice delays. The idea of passing information and documents back and forth with the ease of a button was heavenly, especially when it had previously taken weeks by airmail. Although many of our hosts did not own a fax machine, they could send and receive faxes through their local businesses.

When we moved into the new office, I was fifty-nine. When my parents were my age, they were talking about retirement. I was beginning something new and exciting, directing a ministry and leading people around the world! Times had changed!

As exciting as the growth in the ministry was, Romans 12:1, which says as we seek the Lord we are to make of ourselves a "living sacrifice," took on new meaning. There was a cost to this ministry. I had very little time to spend with my friends and activities outside of MOST Ministries. My focus was narrow: family and ministry.

When the ministry was still new, our youngest son, David, as a sophomore in high school, once interrupted Don and I while at the dinner table by asking, "Is this a family dinner or a ministry meeting?" We realized that we had been deep in a discussion regarding ministry details. He was right; we had allowed our passion for the ministry to crowd out our precious family time. We reassured David that it was indeed a family dinner and were reminded of our need to maintain time for family while responding to the many opportunities and challenges of a growing ministry.

Finding the balance between ministry and family continued to be a juggling act. When my father passed away suddenly and my mother's health began to fail, we placed her in a nursing home in Holland, Michigan, near my brother. Although it was a three hour drive each way, Don and I committed to visiting twice each month.

Over time, I became the face and voice of MOST Ministries causing me to travel to local churches. I explained our need for used eyeglasses and volunteers, encouraging anyone who felt inspired to join a team to heed the call. I had learned that only about one percent of those who hear of short-term missions actually feels a desire to participate. "If you feel inspired to join a team, you may be one of the few." I would say. "Please prayerfully consider if the Lord is speaking to you, encouraging you to take this step."

I was surprised how my new ministry role affected my relationships, especially at church. When members began referring to me as a missionary, I tried to explain that I assisted missionaries and was not one myself, but no one seemed to understand. Eventually, I accepted that I was a missionary of some sort. It was odd how this perception made it difficult for people to act normal around me. Casual conversations became strained and awkward and I began to feel isolated. Thankfully, the new local and international relationships I was forming through the ministry filled the void. It was inspiring to work with our many volunteers and several recently hired staff members—made possible through a Wheat Ridge Foundation grant. I also had the incredible experience of serving beside faith-filled nationals, from Roxanne in Haiti to Dr. Sosars in Latvia. My relationship with Christ also deepened as I learned to rely on Him, doing my best to discern His will through the many decisions I was called on to make.

God continued to lead Eileen; however, this time it was to a husband on staff for Voice of the Martyrs, a wonderful ministry that speaks out on behalf of persecuted Christians around the world. Eileen met her fiancé while leading a MOST Ministries team to serve at their Oklahoma headquarters. I was pleased for her, but sad to see her go. We joked with Eileen, saying that MOST Ministries could now add "match maker" to its list of services.

It wasn't long before the office replaced the electric typewriter with a donated used computer. I loved the benefits, especially e-mail. However, operating it was a disaster for me! As a poor typist my efforts to use the computer were futile and a constant source of frustration. Thankfully, our faithful volunteers took my hand-written letters and e-mails and entered them on the computer.

As the ministry grew, so did its reputation for unique volunteer opportunities. Besides assisting in the office, volunteers packed duffle bags full of supplies for teams, prepared eyeglasses, stuffed mailings, and collated training materials. Returning team members were often eager to volunteer, having appreciated the effort others put forth in preparing their team.

As Don and I laid the foundations for the ministry, we set certain priorities. The top priority was sharing the Christian faith. We understood that the physical assistance we provided to the poor would never bring the life-changing peace that can only be found in Christ. Each of our teams provided an opportunity for the local nationals, pastors and missionaries to share the Good News with those we served. As "second fiddles" that were only there for a short time, we wanted to provide opportunities for the "first violins" to connect with the people and begin a pastoral relationship.

Witness bracelets and tracts were common evangelism tools. We also discovered the EvangeCube (SimplyShareJesus.com). This ingenious picture cube flips and unfolds to reveal a total of seven captivating pictures to help tell the Gospel. I love telling the story while manipulating the cube as it changes shape, surprising the viewers as it opens to reveal more pictures and more of the Good News.

As a ministry we are not only concerned with the faith and well-being of those we serve, but also for those who are serving. We continued to offer the Servanthood Bible Study to help team members prepare spiritually for the act of serving.

What we did not realize during our own early teams to Haiti was how challenging the stress of returning home would be, after so many new experiences. Emotions, thoughts and images rattled around in our heads and hearts after our trips. We did not know how to relate our mission experiences to our family and friends. They couldn't understand, because they hadn't experienced the extreme poverty first-hand, or the genuine joy of the Haitian Christians.

It was after our second team to Haiti that I struggled with this the most. I longed to return to Haiti, not only to help the people, but for selfish reasons. I felt lost at home because I felt God was at work in Haiti, not in Michigan. Often I found myself wishing to return, just to see and feel God more clearly. I felt confused.

I could not stop thinking about the faith-filled lives of the Haitian Christians. The pastor who slept in his damaged church, believing his rubble would someday serve his people, Roxanne, who loved her Savior so dearly that she had chosen to be single for the Lord and the young girl whose leg had grown in response to the pastors' prayers. I was inspired by their faith and dependence on God.

Slowly I began to understand my struggle and strong self-serving desire to return. My daily life in the States did not require me to depend on God in the same way as I had in Haiti. I did not have to pray fervently regarding medicines running out, generators quitting, or the health of those around me. I did not feel as close to God here because I was not relying on Him. The questions finally began to form: how often was I asking God to act in profound ways at home? When He did act, did I give Him the credit, or assume that the blessings I had came from my own doing?

Finally, I identified the real issue and challenge. *How do I, in this land of plenty, live my life completely dependent on God, like the Haitian Christians?* I realized I needed to transfer my longings for Haiti to longings for God. There was a need to seek His presence with fervor, no matter where I was.

It had been good to be challenged, but the process was unsettling. While wrestling through my spiritual issues I also found myself feeling frustrated and annoyed with the typical lifestyle in the United States. I saw the waste of resources and desire for material goods as disturbing. My strong feelings surprised me. Later I learned that other team members also experienced emotional and spiritual struggles when returning home.

> *I needed to transfer my longings for Haiti to longings for God.*

I decided to put together a re-entry workbook. It begins with the question "Who has come home?" Team members look in the mirror, and determine if the person they see is the same as the person who left the country a short time ago.

In another effort to help them process their experiences, team members ask a person to pray for them while they serve. This person is their debriefer (also called Barnabas Buddy) when they return. The debriefer guides the returning team member to process their experiences, using a guide developed by MOST Ministries. Questions like "Was there a time when you were overwhelmed by the poverty?", "How did that affect you?" and "Where did you experience God's presence?" prompts reflection on the mission experience.

As the ministry grew, God led more individuals to become team leaders. Many took on the responsibility while working full-time jobs. The training process took time and diligence. Each leader is required to participate on several teams, at their own expense, and attend extensive training sessions.

These sessions include detailed discussions on topics such as understanding and recognizing culture shock, the importance of understanding the culture where you serve, and the challenge of respecting and following the cultural rules of each country while there.

I knew firsthand the difficulty of understanding the culture. In Ghana I unintentionally dishonored a Ghanaian tribal chief by presenting a gift to him with my left hand. In Ghana, the left hand is the only hand used when toileting, and is considered unclean. The right hand is kept clean for all other tasks.

The gasps that erupted when I extended the gift in my left hand were unforgettable! An unthinkable disgrace! The aide quickly stepped in his chief's place to receive my gift, which was considered a sacrificial act on his part.

Realizing my mistake I continued the presentation with my left hand behind my back, demonstrating my recognition of my error and attempting to show them I would not repeat such an offense. They seemed to accept my unspoken apology, but I had learned a valuable lesson. I would never make that mistake again! I would learn the cultural rules and nuances, and follow them!

Besides knowing the culture, it is critical that teams focus on safety. Each team leader is required to have a current First Aid Certification and to understand what to do in emergencies. Before each team is sent, the ministry develops a plan of action to be taken in any given crisis. Each team member is registered with the local embassy, providing the team leader with easy access to emergency responses.

A trained nurse or medic goes out with each team. At home, Dr. Carroll, a specialist in international medicine for short-term mission teams, is available by phone 24/7 to respond to more serious medical conditions, having been supplied with each team member's medical history.

MOST Ministries continued to grow at an incredible rate. In 2001 we had four full-time staff members and had moved into a six-room building, still on Concordia College's campus. With a total of ten team leaders, including myself, and the increase in staff, MOST Ministries was able to send out eleven teams that year, serving in five different countries.

After joining a 2001 eyeglass team an optician returned convinced that the ministry would benefit greatly by owning its own edger. An edger could trace the frame of any pair of glasses and then cut a new lens, making a perfect fit. Don and I did not fully understand the importance of this machine to our ministry, but were grateful for his enthusiasm and suggestion. Trusting his professional opinion and not wanting to lag behind if God inspired this, we applied for and received grant monies to help us purchase a used edger.

The operation of this machinery was challenging. Thankfully, several retired engineers, committed to volunteering for the ministry, were successful in learning to cut lenses. We soon understood the value of this machine. It allowed us to make use of the hundreds of frames with unusable prescriptions. We could now remove the old lenses and cut our own new lenses with the prescription strengths needed most often on the field.

We also added the staff position of Volunteer Coordinator. An enthusiastic woman, Lynn, joined our staff and took on the responsibility of organizing the wonderful men and women that arrived at the office, eager to help. She used the new office space to expand our volunteer opportunities even further by recruiting and scheduling church groups to participate in well-organized activities. We began receiving vans full of church members, some traveling an hour to serve us.

They arrived at the office eager to participate in tasks like washing and preparing eyeglasses. While they worked, Lynn shared inspiring stories from the field. The volunteers left knowing their efforts would have an impact around the world.

With the ability to create a well-stocked inventory of eyeglasses, the hiring of a volunteer coordinator, and an increase in available team leaders, our eyeglass ministry blossomed and grew. As was so often the case when we were content with the status quo, God acted miraculously, showing He had even greater plans for the ministry. We had been sending out an average of two to three eyeglass teams a year, but we now had the resources and means to schedule six eyeglass teams to be sent out in 2002, triple the number of eyeglass teams that went out in 2001.

When Don and I organized the first team to Haiti, short-term missions was non-existent, at least to our knowledge, within our religious denomination, the Lutheran Church Missouri Synod (LCMS). In order to participate on a team, we looked beyond our church denomination. As our ministry grew, we continued to have a relationship with the LCMS in the hopes of encouraging short-term missions within this body of believers, knowing the amazing spiritual benefits to all involved. Over time, MOST Ministries developed a relationship with the Lutheran Church Missouri Synod and in 2001 we achieved the honored status of a Recognized Service Organization (RSO) within the denomination.

With this partnership word spread quickly within the Lutheran church at large, helping more individuals learn of opportunities to serve and grow through short-term missions. This also opened doors for Lutheran missionaries and partner churches around the world to contact us, requesting teams. It seemed that everywhere I turned, there were signs of growth.

The tragic events of September 11, 2001 brought everything to a standstill. Our nation watched with horror as airliners struck the Twin Towers, then gasped as they crumbled. The use of airliners as weapons caused the whole nation to rethink air travel. With a ministry based on travel, we felt the effects. It was difficult for our team members to remain committed to their teams scheduled to depart shortly after the tragedy. We understood the concerns, as we all wondered, *will it happen again?* No one knew.

There was a sharp decline in teams in the beginning of 2002 and we became fearful of the long-term effects on the ministry, but eventually the nation regained its faith in the safety of flight, trusting the government's new security measures for travelers. Teams continued to press on, including all six of the previously scheduled eyeglass teams. In 2002 we sent a total of sixteen teams into the field, serving ten different countries.

Don and I were never alone in leading the ministry. The Board of Directors was our safety net as they guided the ministry with Godly wisdom. I often felt they were like Aaron, who held up Moses' arms.

They gave me strength during difficult times and were always a source of encouragement.

It is hard to believe that in the beginning the ministry operated without the help of personal copy machines, fax machines, computers, scanners, cell phones and the Internet. As each new technology became available, our effectiveness increased and the ministry broadened.

In 2003 a volunteer, another woman with the name Eileen, enjoyed selling personal items on eBay and noticed vintage eyeglasses offered on the site. She asked if she might try selling some of the antique wire frames donated to MOST as a source of revenue for our ministry. The glasses did sell, and for good prices. This inspired her to continue. Our volunteer sorters were soon instructed on the types of glasses to set aside to be sold on eBay. What a creative form of ministry this woman began! The proceeds from her sales initially averaged a few thousand a year, and then it really took off. Before we knew it she was averaging over $15,000 annually!

Eileen sold to buyers near and far. Expensive used sunglasses were even shipped to a member of a rock band for a photo shoot! Aviator pilot sunglasses have been sent to the military of Brazil and Israel. In Thailand they order gold rim glasses.

For Eileen the eBay sales have become more than just a way to support MOST Ministries. It is a ministry by itself. Every description of eyeglasses on eBay ends with two Bible verses. Every box that is sent through the mail has an orange sticker with a picture of the world, saying, "In the beginning, GOD created the Heavens and the earth." (Genesis 1:1). It was exciting to watch as God led Eileen to use her unique talents and interests to create her own special blend of service and ministry.

As more and more individuals like Eileen felt called by God to serve MOST Ministries at home or on teams, the ministry grew. In 2005 we sent out twenty-seven teams to thirteen different countries with over 400 people participating on these teams. Over 7,900 people received eyeglasses with more than 12,000 people served over all. By this time we had provided teams to a total of twenty-eight different countries, including China, Cote d'Ivoire, Indonesia, Poland, India,

Bolivia, Brazil, Honduras, Nicaragua, Puerto Rico, Venezuela, Slovakia, Tanzania, and Russia. We listened to the requests from the field, and provided an ever-growing variety of teams, including Teacher Training, Geriatric Seminars, Marriage Retreats, Evangelism Events, Vacation Bible Schools, Sanitation and many more.

Don and I were amazed at how far MOST Ministries had come, from a home office to a six-room building with a devoted staff! We marveled at the ever-increasing number of teams MOST Ministries was sending around the world.

We were always quick to recognize that ministry growth happened through God's leadership, not ours. He worked within the hearts of many individuals, leading them to serve through MOST Ministries. Our staff, board of directors, team leaders, team members and volunteers all expressed feeling guided by God to serve Him through this ministry. With each passing year, as the ministry grew, Don and I remained in awe and continued to wonder, *what* are *God's plans for MOST Ministries?*

Haiti, A Land of Grace

My heart was filled with joy as we laughed and sang while making these "flags".

Roxanne, single for the Lord, carrying a cement block to the work site.

Walking along this ditch on the path to Roxanne's was terrifying.

Cite Soleil pastor, and the banner from the reconstruction team, which brightens the newly refurbished church.

Hundreds of hopeful Haitians arrive early to secure a "ticket" for the doctor's exam.

God's Precious Gifts

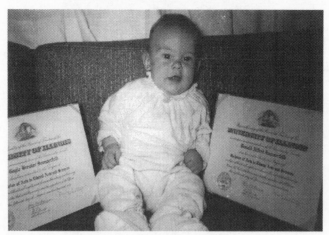

Our newborn son, Scott Gordon, between our hard-earned college diplomas.

La Gonave medical team, Don and twins, Gina and Ginnel, from listless to alert.

Morning prayers with Jesus. His presence drew me close to Him and filled my soul.

A Simple Test, Profound Results

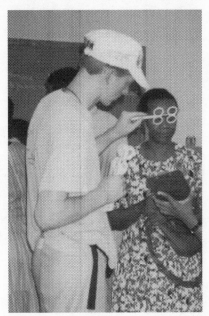

In Haiti, David, our tall 17 year old son. As a male, he was regarded with high authority on the testing team.

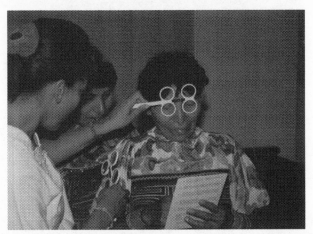

In Panama, using flippers for testing, this Kuna Indian will be blessed with improved sight.

Inspiring and Menacing Monuments

Latvian Freedom Monument, a symbol of hope that survived decades of Russian Occupation.

Russian Rifleman Monument. Huge and menacing, the three stone soldiers standing back to back give the appearance of power as they look down on the citizens of Latvia.

Russian Brutality and Propaganda

A mother uses the magnifying glass to see the Scriptures on the reading test. Her nearly blind daughter stands behind her.

A room overflowing with Russian propaganda is ready to be removed and destroyed. This evil was replaced with compassion from the doctors of the new Christian Medical and Family Center.

Part Two

Impacting the World

My adventures with God and Mission Opportunities Short Term (MOST Ministries) continued to take me around the world. Don often remained at home contributing to our support while expanding the eyeglass ministry. One team visit regularly led to another as nationals and missionaries continued to request our help.

What follows are selected highlights from my personal experiences, organized by global regions and ministry emphases. Each chapter is chronological, but new regions and chapters may reset to the time when MOST Ministries first began working in that region.

These stories are not intended to make a statement about current affairs in foreign lands. Time has passed since my travels, allowing laws and customs to change. Rather, they are the accounts of what I experienced during the time I was there. These narratives celebrate God's greatness and reveal what can be accomplished when ordinary people respond to His calling.

Latvia

and

Kyrgyzstan

15

From Callous to Compassionate

Latvia

Less than a year after our 1993 eyeglass team to Latvia, MOST Ministries received an invitation to return. The request was for a construction team to refurbish an old school, generously donated to the church by the new Latvian government. We were also asked to provide an eyeglass clinic in Sloka, a city just outside of Riga.

Our new team consisted of several professionals, including a doctor, dentist, and two teachers. The doctor and dentist would speak to the Latvian medical communities. The teachers were invited to visit the schools and nursing homes to tell flannelgraph Bible stories. Steve, who was now training to be a team leader, would join me as an assistant. We had five different ministry goals. Although the trip was ultimately a success, it was a good learning experience in being stretched too thin in too many places. After this mission, we kept our focus to one or two acts of service per trip.

It was September 1994 when our team of fifteen individuals was bussed to our lodging in Sloka, which had comfortable beds and private baths, where we would stay for ten days. Steve took the construction team members out to begin refurbishing the old school. Unfortunately, just as we experienced in Haiti, the needed materials did not arrive and the team was redirected. They transitioned smoothly to their new project: to repair and paint the local Sloka church.

Everyone was surprised by the choice of color for the exterior—bright green! It was a bold statement, I thought, for the formerly drab Latvia under the Soviet regime, but then I remembered the brightly colored facades of Old Town and realized that Latvians love color.

While several team members painted the exterior, others used the interior rooms to provide a two-day eyeglass clinic. It was a joy to once again serve the Latvians. They waited patiently and were incredibly grateful; offering us hugs and smiles when they received their glasses. In the end we cared for over two hundred people. While we met their vision needs we were troubled to learn of the many other medical needs this nation faced.

Our dentist spoke at the local dental school, discussing updated techniques to common procedures. His lectures went well, but what most captured his personal interest was a young girl we met at the local church who was born without an arm. We learned that she was adopted and that her deformity was most likely a birth defect caused by the 1986 Chernobyl nuclear disaster. Sadly, Russia, Latvia and other neighboring countries had experienced an increase in birth defects and anomalies following the tragic nuclear meltdown.

Our dentist discussed the young girl's need for a prosthetic arm with the Latvian medical community. He was discouraged to learn that very few Latvians had access to prosthetics. He felt a heavy burden for those in need of such assistance, but there was nothing that our team could do during our short visit.

This story had a happy ending, however. At the end of the trip, our dentist returned home inspired to help provide Latvians with prosthetics. He continued in his pursuits outside of MOST Ministries. He was successful in helping the little girl receive a prosthetic arm. He also returned to Latvia to help train doctors in creating prosthetics as well as inviting them to the U.S. for specialized training. God is so creative; he can call a dentist to provide prosthetics! It was encouraging for me to think of the good he was doing and how it started with our MOST Ministries team.

The biggest change in Latvian medicine was yet to come. Dr. Fox, a team member, spoke to the medical community at the largest cancer hospital in the Latvian nation. During his presentation Dr. Fox mentioned the benefits of hospice care, a philosophy that encourages compassionate care for the dying. Dr. Sosars, a Latvian oncologist who had assisted us on our first team, listened intently. He was acquainted with the hospice practice, also referred to as palliative care in neighboring nations. Dr. Sosars wished to bring this medical model to the freed Latvians.

The communist view of the body had been cold and heartless. They considered people to be machines with no emotions or soul. This was the philosophy in which Dr. Sosars' colleagues had been trained. He hoped and prayed that with a new government would come a new medical philosophy, one filled with compassion towards the human body and soul, like the hospice model.

Under communist rule doctors had been told that when the body was too broken to fix, it was to be discarded. No assistance was given to the dying patient or to their families. Why waste pain medications on a person who could no longer be a productive citizen? They even allowed euthanasia. Suffering in silence was to be expected. I thought it sounded like death by abandonment.

When I asked Dr. Sosars how MOST Ministries could continue to serve the Latvians, he shared his desire to introduce his colleagues to the hospice philosophy. He asked if our ministry would consider returning with a hospice training team. Several of us gathered to discuss and pray about his request. I had no personal knowledge of hospice or palliative care, but I trusted that if this was God's desire, He would lead us.

After I returned home, I began researching hospice and palliative care. I learned that both practices are founded on the goal of keeping the patient comfortable and meeting their needs. In the United States the term "palliative care" is considered care given during any prolonged illness, usually in a hospital or long-term care facility. Hospice care refers to the care given nearing the end of life and can include home care. However, as I discussed the topic with the Latvians, I learned that in many foreign countries and to the Latvians, the term "palliative care" seemed to encompass both prolonged illness and end of life care.

In both practices the patient is the center of all decisions. The hospice model used in the United States provides the patient with a team of professionals consisting of a doctor, nurse, social worker, psychologist and chaplain to walk beside them. This program guides the patient through important issues to consider, like the profoundly emotional healing process of reconciliation with family members. It also provides insight into the spiritual nature of man and reassurance of a forgiving God. I was encouraged by the open discussions of faith that were an integral part of this program and appreciated how it offered assistance to the grieving family.

The more I learned, the more committed I became to forming a team. I began recruiting skilled professionals certified in hospice training and was especially encouraged when I contacted Dr. Hergt, who founded a hospice program in Michigan. He was eager to join the team and share his expertise.

Forming this team had been unusually challenging, which caused me to wonder with excitement, *what does God have planned for Latvia and hospice care?* I knew that struggles often preceded acts of God's greatness!

Our new team of hospice-trained professionals arrived in Latvia in September 1995, a year after the original request. As we drove to our lodging, I could see that the stone soldiers of the Riflemen Monument still stood guard near the Christian Medical and Family Center, a symbolic reminder of Latvia's troubled past, but this time the streets were lively and new shops had opened. Women wore popular new European styles. They walked with confidence, their heads held high, even offering an occasional smile! Astra, our Latvian interpreter from America on our first trip to Latvia, was with us again. She was encouraged to see her countrymen adjusting well to their freedoms.

Our hospice seminars were held in a large auditorium on the hospital grounds. It was exciting to watch seventy doctors and nurses eagerly pick up their lecture materials as they entered the auditorium.

They listened receptively to the lectures, quickly discarding the Soviet's cold and calculating view of the body while acknowledging the patient's emotional and spiritual needs. They welcomed the idea of working with a chaplain and social worker to assist the patient and their families.

When our seminar came to an end, we awarded seventy certificates of Palliative Care training. These doctors and nurses, however, were not satisfied. They hungered for more and asked us to return the next year. We agreed.

A dedicated group of participants also formed the Latvian Palliative Care Association, hoping to work with the new government to officially approve palliative care for Latvian hospitals. It was not a surprise when they elected Dr. Sosars as chairman.

The following year in September 1996 a second MOST Ministries hospice training team returned to Latvia with four North American team members. Dr. Sosars had also extended invitations to professionals from Poland, Lithuania and Austria to make presentations. Dr. Hergt, who was on the first hospice team, led MOST's small team. One hundred and eighty certificates were presented at this now international event, dubbed the Second Annual Hospice Conference.

In 1997 our third and last MOST Ministries Latvia hospice training team gave a final seminar in Latvia for medical professionals, social work students and spiritual leaders. Rev. James Jasper, a chaplain from the famous Cleveland Clinic, opened the presentations using an overhead projector to show several beautiful classical artworks that depicted individuals facing death surrounded by loved ones. He strummed an autoharp as he spoke. It was mesmerizing.

He stopped the music as the last picture was displayed. The room was silent. It was a modern stained glass artwork of a woman connected to IV bags, not connected to people, but dying alone in a very sterile hospital environment. It clearly showed the need for human contact and support as death approaches.

The next day we presented at the Attistiba School of Social Work. There were over one hundred students crowded in the classroom, spilling out into the hallways, listening as best they could. Rev. Jasper began the seminar with the same classical artworks and the impact was profound. Students were eager to learn how to assist and comfort the dying.

We were surprised when the Attistiba staff requested that Rev. Jasper, and not our social worker, return the next day to continue the discussion. Russians, who had been closely associated with the communist party in the past, staffed this private school. They did not incorporate the spiritual nature of man into their curriculum, so it was interesting to us that they just requested the return of the minister. It was evident that his presentation had affected them deeply.

Fortunately, the local Bishops' conference center provided plenty of space for the many pastors and priests who attended the Hospice Chaplaincy training. We were told that this was the first interdenominational gathering since Latvia's independence. The excitement of the participants was palpable. The hospice training opened doors for these men of faith to discuss the many issues surrounding death and comforting the dying, and gave them tools to assist in the hospice program and to minister to their congregations by effectively comforting those who are dying or grieving.

Within three years MOST Ministries had successfully provided three hospice-training teams. During that time the Latvian Palliative Care Association was successful in working with the new government in acquiring funds to provide for palliative care units in all of Latvia's hospitals! We were also encouraged to hear that they planned to include hospice training in their curriculum and that the Latvian Palliative Care Association would continue holding training seminars. As we rejoiced with them, we were not only celebrating the changes in medicine, but also in their country. Wounds were healing.

Our greatest excitement was participating in the dedication of a newly opened twenty-five bed hospice unit in the largest hospital in Riga. This unit also included a chapel that allowed patients to be wheeled in their beds or wheelchairs for Sunday services. It provided a place for quiet contemplation in a spiritual setting. A chaplain, trained through our seminars, was on staff to pray and comfort patients and their families.

When the others left for home, Astra and I remained for a few extra days and attended a local church's first baptismal service since their independence. As I listened to the beautiful Latvian hymns in the bone-chilling cold of the old stone church, I thought of the pain of those who had endured the initial silencing of faith a half century ago. I watched, filled with a mixture of sadness for the past and joy for the future, as whole families were baptized. Those who had endured the long sentence of silence wept, their joy impossible to contain, while their children and grandchildren publicly professed their faith. Astra and I wept as well.

I returned home grateful for my freedoms and thankful for the changes happening in Latvia. Its medical centers were now providing palliative care: offering a way for patients to come before God in peace and comfort. It was a miraculous transformation from the previous communist philosophy of soulless human beings who were nothing but machines, to a country open to baptism and public professions of faith. What a contrast!

16

Would You Like a Blessing?

Kyrgyzstan

I am too sick, Lord, I said between coughing spells *I just can't go.* That was my plea when I went to the doctor's office, less than a day before my scheduled departure to Kyrgyzstan.

It was 2001 and we were responding to a request for palliative care and hospice training. Several of the same experienced individuals who had been involved in the Latvia hospice training teams, including Dr. Sosars, were on this team. A capable group that could manage without me, I hoped. I felt horrible, too sick to make a twenty-three hour trek across the Atlantic and then be an effective team leader when arriving in Bishkek, the capital city.

As I coughed violently during the examination, I was sure I would be given a medical excuse. That would be the answer to my 'don't send me' plea. Instead, the nurse came into the exam room with an air of conviction and simply stated that I was going to go. God would bless my efforts, she declared, and she would be lighting a candle and saying a novena, a special nine-day series of prayer, for me at mass in her Catholic church. I tried to dissuade her and impress on her how ill I was, but she was insistent. With strong medication and her petition to God, she was sure my needs would be met.

Reluctantly, I packed my medication and my bags. Thankfully, I was able to rest for a significant portion of the trip. Arriving in slightly better condition than the previous day, I thought of the nurse and her promise of prayers.

When the Lutheran Compassion Ministry in Bishkek, Kyrgyzstan first made its request for a hospice training team, I had to grab my globe to search for this country. I had never heard of it. I learned it is a small, landlocked nation bordered by China and other countries with which I was equally unfamiliar: Kazakhstan, Tajikistan and Uzbekistan.

When I discovered Kyrgyzstan was a former communist country, I knew there would be a definite need to bring the hospice teachings to these people. Kyrgyzstan had deep Russian and Soviet roots. It became a part of the Russian Empire in the late 1800's, which eventually led to joining the Soviet Union. I wondered what this country would be like, having shared a similar past to Latvia. Would I sense the differences or similarities? Had the Kyrgyz, like the Latvians, been successful in leaving their communist roots behind? I truly hoped so.

Our materials were sent ahead for translation into Russian, the common language, for the 125 attendees. We hoped to prepare them for our team's presentation, which would mean a radical change in their care for the dying.

We descended over Bishkek, a picturesque city, nestled in a vast mountain range. Yurts, circular tent-like structures made from heavy woolen felt, dotted the mountainside. These were the homes of the nomadic Kyrgyz who traveled the mountains, tending to their sheep, yaks, goats, and camels.

Bishkek was a large city. The Russian influence was evident in many of the Stalinist block style buildings. As we drove to our lodging, I could not stop staring at the men on the streets. They wore tall white felt hats with black trim. It looked like a Kyrgyz version of the stovepipe top hat! Other than the hats, their clothing was similar to our own. The women wore slacks and skirts but no jeans.

Our team reached the comfortable apartment provided for our stay to find the Kyrgyz had gifted us with a pair of felt slippers for each team member. The Kyrgyz were very proud of their felt. It was made from natural woolen fibers and was much thicker and stronger than our North American synthetic felt. It was a special and prized product of this country and had many uses.

Our hosts, Tim and Rita Nickels, were missionaries who empathized with the Kyrgyz and their struggles to recover from communism. They desired, just as Dr. Sosars had in Latvia, to encourage the medical community to embrace the human need for love and compassion, especially during the end of life. We could not hold a conference without government approval. They worked diligently to obtain permission for physicians and nurses to attend our seminar.

We were honored when government officials began the Hospice Training Conference with a short ceremony. Several officials welcomed and thanked our team. The Minister of Health even spoke, making this amazing statement: "This medical conference is the first to be held in Kyrgyzstan since the Russian occupation ended in 1991, one decade ago." I was stunned. I had not been aware of the significance of our event.

It was also disappointing. *How could it be that this country was still so isolated?* I realized the incredible hunger these doctors and nurses had for outside information. They eagerly digested all of the information we offered. Basic things, such as images of common cancerous tumors that are readily available in the United States, were new to these professionals.

During the last session there was a core group of thirty-five Kyrgyz doctors and nurses who shared their desire to bring this new hospice philosophy into their hospitals. We were overjoyed, and even more excited when Dr. Sosars committed himself as a future contact for the hospitals. What a perfect match! He spoke fluent Russian and had several years of experience with introducing hospice care.

We hoped they also had a hunger for learning about the spiritual nature of man. For many, this was the first time they heard a clear presentation explaining why Christians have hope in the afterlife, not only presented by the chaplain but also explained in Russian in their syllabus.

After the sessions ended, I was saddened as I walked the public streets. Hopelessness hung in the air like a dark cloud. The people wore blank looks, clouded stares, no smiles. It felt similar to my first visit to Latvia.

Only the Christians seemed joyful, but while we were encouraged to learn that Christianity was growing, we were concerned. The Taliban were killing Christians in the south and were rumored to be moving towards Bishkek. Those who became Christians knew the possibility of persecution, but having been spiritually starved during the communist era, they were now hungry for spiritual truth and willing to sacrifice for it.

Throughout the conference we were aware of another kind of hunger. We provided lunch for the attendees between seminars, as we typically do, yet the doctors and nurses ate so much and so quickly, it was as though the food simply vanished. Mentioning my surprise to the host, she explained that the doctors do not typically have lunch because they can't afford to eat three meals a day. This meal was a blessing for these very hungry people. Each day I ordered more food and added delicacies like fruit to the menu. Each day I witnessed the same ravenous response.

Shocked and saddened, I learned that the medical staff is grossly underpaid. Originally trained by the Russians, who bragged that there were more Russian doctors per capita than in the West, there was now an overabundance of doctors, resulting in low wages. Kyrgyzstan was slow to recover from the communist philosophies. There were no private practices. They were all trained and sent to work in government hospitals, usually for life. This was also true of other professions and for the general population. There appeared to be no private businesses; almost everything was still owned by the government.

The needs in Kyrgyzstan were great. We arranged with our hosts for an eyeglass team to return the following year. This team would train an evangelist, a local Christian Kyrgyz, to test and fit eyeglasses. She would then travel with an existing mobile medical clinic, an outreach of the Lutheran Compassion Ministry. This would expand their services, enabling them to provide eyeglasses as they traveled to local and nomadic communities. Steve, a skilled team leader by now, would lead this future team.

When I left Kyrgyzstan, I was angry with God for the unjust situation in that country and its slow recovery from the communist influences, resulting in poverty of body and spirit. This was similar to early Latvia, but in Latvia, I had watched as the country recovered and improved with each year. Here, it was as though the country had just been liberated. No progress had been made in the past ten years. The people continued to suffer.

I lashed out at God, asking, *"How could You allow this?"* I packed my bags eager to return home and was irritated when I remembered that our itinerary included an overnight in London. I was ready to be in familiar settings, away from this disturbing place.

My frustration at God increased when I paid a London taxi driver more to take us to the hotel than I had paid in Kyrgyzstan for a large restaurant meal for over twenty people. How could the cultures of the world be so different? It all seemed unfair for those who lacked so much. I climbed into bed, with a tirade of thoughts all aimed at God and the injustice I witnessed.

Finally, God broke through my angry internal banter. *"Do you want to crab and complain all night or would you like a blessing?"* Surprised and confused by the intrusion into my thoughts, I humbly chose "blessing" and stopped my internal ranting which allowed me to finally drift off to sleep.

The next day, we decided to visit Westminster Abbey during our layover in London. I entered to the sound of glorious singing, the kind that fills your soul. It echoed from a distant chamber. Leaving the group, I was drawn to the music and desperately tried to find the source. I walked through a maze of grottos and statues. Eventually I found it, a worship service in a small chapel, but by the time I arrived, it had already ended and everyone was leaving; I was bitterly disappointed. The priest, seeing my response, invited me to come forward and kneel at the altar as he was leaving. I accepted his invitation.

Kneeling there I was overcome with thoughts of the great Christian men and women who had gone before me, filling me with a sense that I was on hallowed ground. I was not sure how much time passed as I lingered there, but during that time my anger towards God that had weighed so heavily on me was gently lifted off my shoulders. My spirit was healed and filled with a quiet joy as I realized I was receiving, within these hallowed halls, the blessing I had chosen the night before. Although I had grumbled about the long layover in London, God knew I needed to experience His grace before continuing my journey home and my journey with Him.

Seeing the pain and suffering of so many people groups around this fragile world, such as that in Kyrgyzstan, was often emotionally draining. Although I had received the "blessing" in London, and my spirit thankfully returned to a place of peace, I was no closer to understanding the ever present question of "why?"

I knew that if I had stayed in that place of anger, I would have been paralyzed by bitterness, unable to continue moving forward as God led. My calling was to go and serve, to bring willing volunteers around the world to be God's hands and feet, enabling our many hosts to provide for those in their care. How could I question God when He revealed His greatness to me daily through miraculous circumstances? Eventually I realized, my role was not to fully understand, but to *fully trust.*

... my role was not to fully understand, but to fully trust.

17

Rippling Effects

Latvia

After my struggles in Kyrgyzstan, God encouraged me through two special glimpses of the long-term effects of our short-term teams. In 2001 Don and I chose to take a much-needed vacation. Having accrued ample points with the airlines, we chose to return to Riga, Latvia. This city and nation had captured our hearts. We were excited to return to the city which was now celebrating its 800th anniversary.

While there we walked the busy streets. The atmosphere throughout Old Town was festive, with crowds of visitors ready to celebrate this historic occasion. The streets were filled with joy and laughter.

We eagerly made our way back to the old stone building, the home of the Christian Medical and Family Center. Unfortunately, we were too late; the building was closed for the night. We stood there recalling our former teams. So many memories! Just as we were about to leave and return the next day, the director unexpectedly exited out of one of the doors! He was shocked to see us and we were all in awe of this coincidence of perfect timing, clearly prearranged by God. We greeted one another and he warmly welcomed us into the building, proudly giving us a tour of the clinic.

The greatest joy was when we stepped inside the welcoming and brightly lit room dedicated to the permanent eyeglass clinic. It was a fully-functioning well-stocked eye clinic, posting regular hours for exams several days a week. Display boards filled with a variety of glasses lined the wall, ready for patients to make a selection. One of the volunteers, who happened to be working late that evening, enthusiastically explained his responsibilities for repairing the broken frames. He thanked us over and over again for our part in providing the poor people of Latvia with free glasses.

From its early conception Don, being called and led by God, had nurtured and guided this eyeglass ministry. Now, standing in the middle of this room there was a deep sense of satisfaction and joy as God revealed just one of the many results from his faithful service. We could see that the MOST Ministries teams were like a single drop of water in the communities where they served, creating a ripple effect that often extended far beyond what we could see or imagine.

While we were encouraged by this encounter, God was not finished rejuvenating our spirits. There were more stories to hear of the positive impacts of MOST Ministries teams in Latvia.

The next day Don and I met with a dear Latvian friend, Rev. Dauksts, in an outdoor café. He had participated in the Hospice Chaplaincy training many years earlier and then requested an English as a Second Language (ESL) team as a camp outreach for his church. The camp was so successful that MOST Ministries has continued to send ESL teams annually to Latvia to serve Rev. Dauksts.

Together, Rev. Dauksts and MOST Ministries organize and run a weeklong summer camp in the nearby countryside where Latvian children and adults practice their conversational English. MOST Ministries team members come prepared to use Bible stories to teach all levels of English, from beginner to advanced placement.

Rev. Dauksts was pleased to see us and eager to share how an ESL team helped open doors for him to begin ministering to local orphan boys, fathered by Russian soldiers. When Russia withdrew in 1991, the fathers returned to Russia. While Latvians derived a person's citizenship through the father, Russian citizenship is through the mother. These boys could not obtain citizenship in either country. Legally, they did not exist, having no documents proving their nationality. These boys became the untouchables, the outcasts of modern Latvia.

Each year Rev. Dauksts picks a new location for the MOST Ministries-led ESL camp. This past year the camp shared space with a local orphanage. Campers and orphans dined in the same hall, but the orphan outcasts sat alone, never interacting with the others.

The orphan boys were intrigued, however, and watched the ESL camp activities from a distance. They observed as the campers and the team members sang songs together and joined hands in prayer. At first, when the American team members made eye contact and offered welcoming smiles, the orphan boys looked away. They were shy but over time they began returning the smiles. Eventually, the boys sat closer and closer to the teaching areas while listening to the engaging Bible stories.

The teams' welcoming gestures opened the door for Rev. Dauksts to speak to the boys. He sought them out in the evenings and shared about Jesus and His love. Rev. Dauksts, having been forced to serve in the Soviet army before he came to Christ, had experienced hardship and loneliness himself. He knew how lost one could be without the love of Christ and he hoped to offer these orphans a sense of belonging as a member of Christ's family.

The tradition for the last night of the ESL camp was to gather around a bonfire and make s'mores. The orphan boys were intrigued by this American treat and they could not resist. By the end of the evening all were gathered around the bonfire for prayer, even the orphan boys. They found a warm welcome, something they rarely experienced.

As Don and I listened intently to Rev. Dauksts tell us about the camp and the orphans, we were overjoyed when he ended this happy tale with even more good news. Shortly after the camp the boys had traveled into the city to look for him, asking about Jesus and requesting instruction for baptism! He eagerly agreed, welcoming them into the church family.

Several of these boys were in trouble with the law and awaiting judgments from the courts. They were thankful for Rev. Dauksts' support and friendship during this stressful time. Having only known the harsh law of the land, they were now discovering the grace of a forgiving Savior and the love of a Christian brother.

Don and I returned to the States refreshed and inspired. Seeing the permanent eyeglass clinic and hearing about the life-changing effects of the ministry for the young orphan boys left me in awe of God. Never in a million years would I have imagined the many creative ways He would use our teams, far beyond what Don and I had hoped. It was exciting to hear that lives were touched and changed, even after each team's departure.

I was eager to continue to follow God's lead as we scheduled more teams. I was learning that it was my job to allow Christ to lead me and the ministry, not to question His paths throughout the world.

It was around this time that I discovered the poem *Pedal*, written by an anonymous author. I appreciated the imagery and felt it brought to life the very lessons I had been learning, to surrender and trust. The poem begins:

> When I first met Christ
> It seemed as though life was rather like a bike ride,
> But it was a tandem bike,
> And I noticed that Christ
> Was in the back helping me pedal.
>
> I don't know just when it was that
> He suggested we change places,
> But life has not been the same since...

The author goes on to share the initial struggle the rider experienced while relinquishing control, a struggle I remembered well from my own life. As Jesus steers the rider down new paths, in directions they would never have chosen on their own, the rider learns to trust and finds great joy and peace in the journey, even when the path is challenging. I imagined Don and I pedaling our bikes as Christ led MOST Ministries around the world. We were doing our best to trust as He took us over rocky paths that were difficult and at times overwhelming. Yet we both would agree that those were often the paths that led to stunning views and life changing moments.

I remembered one especially challenging "ride." It was shortly after our second team to Latvia in 1994. MOST Ministries had been invited to serve in the city of Hong Kong. Initially the preparations went smoothly; then suddenly this team's path took such a jarring turn that it was all I could do to hang on and see where in the world the Lord was *really* leading us!

Macau

and

China

18

Who Will Take Us?

Macau

Lord, I have twelve tickets to Hong Kong and twelve committed team members. Now, with only ten days until departure, the project and plans have been cancelled!

I was frantic as I cried out to God. *With no host, we have nowhere to stay and no one to serve.* I had spent months making the arrangements. *Who will take us? What will we do?*

It was the summer of 1994. Our flights were to the city of Hong Kong, a city and country that was still a democracy under British rule.

During the early months of preparation I had watched a video about Hong Kong, created by the Lutheran church. It spoke of the many wonderful ministries in this Asian nation, which remained open to the gospel unlike neighboring China. It featured Lois, an American deaconess using flannelgraph felt figures to tell Bible stories to children, something I enjoy. Our original plans did not include any contact with the local churches. After seeing Lois's love for the children, I felt strongly that I wanted to connect with her. I prayed that I would have an opportunity to meet her while I was in the country.

This was long before our current crisis. Now, I desperately reached out to the Lutheran church administration, wondering if any of their ministries in Hong Kong could take on the heavy responsibility of housing our team and providing us with a service opportunity.

The director of a Lutheran School for the Deaf invited us to serve and stay at their school. We would be doing odd jobs like cataloguing the library and making repairs in the classrooms. Lois, knowing nothing about my desire to meet her, happened to be in the Hong Kong office that day and heard about our needs. She offered to assist the director in hosting our group! My prayers had been answered; not only did we have a destination, but I would be working with Lois.

The school we were to serve was not in Hong Kong, but in the neighboring Portuguese colony of Macau, a small peninsula off of mainland China. Macau encouraged foreign visitors and travel, so no special visas were required. The small colony was only a short ferry ride from Hong Kong. We agreed to the new mission.

The team arrived in Hong Kong after an exhausting international flight. Lois greeted us warmly and transported us to the ferry for our final destination. It was dark when we arrived in the city of Macau. Although Macau was once a thriving port, connecting the East to the West, today it was a city noted for its casinos: the "Monte Carlo" of the Orient.

It was late at night when we finally arrived at the school. I was impressed with the staff's creativity. The classrooms had been hastily transformed into dormitories, with plywood placed across the tops of the student's desks. We were grateful for the addition of a very thin foam mattress. Exhausted we climbed onto our "beds."

Lois, Eileen, and I shared a sturdy ping pong table. I was afraid I'd fall off! When I suggested to the director that we put our mattress on the floor, he told me that they were in the process of exterminating mice. The floor was a bad idea.

The school was closed for the week, so we would not be interacting with the students, but there would be a picnic on the last day where we could meet the students we had served. At this time in Macau deaf children were not taught in the regular school system. Traditionally they were hidden away by their parents out of shame. The Christian school offered them an education and opportunities to enter society as a valued member.

Our projects were simple and after the work sessions we ventured out into the surrounding neighborhood. The crowds were overwhelming which made it difficult to navigate the sidewalks as we made our way to the marketplace. When we finally arrived, many unusual sights, sounds and smells greeted us. There were delicious-looking pastries. There were also strange-looking meats, including cooked chicken feet on a stick, which they ate as we might eat a corn dog!

I loved being immersed in the culture, however, I was not prepared for my visit to the Buddhist Temple. I entered a tall cavernous room, filled with smoke from large hanging incense coils. Their soot made thin coverings on all the stone Buddhas and their lesser gods. Sacrifices of fresh foods were placed in front of the idols. Lois explained that often people left fruit, cooked chickens and other edibles for these stone gods. Others worshipped their ancestors by purchasing paper money, printed with the words "Bank of Hell," and placed them in a special brick pit with a blazing fire.

In addition to paper money the temple store sold many other paper items to burn, such as almost life-sized flat paper clothing, jewelry, TV's and much more. These were purchased and burned, believing the vapors transported the items to their ancestors in the afterlife, which they referred to as hell. Those offering the sacrifices feared that if their dead ancestors were not properly honored and provided for, they might let the living know of their need by causing mischief in their lives here on earth. I watched as homage and sacrifices were paid out of fear to these gods and spirits, similar to the voodoo worship in Haiti.

It was distressing to watch the people spend their money and waste their food on these gods and dead ancestors. These stone gods could provide no comfort for those who petitioned them. How could they have compassion? Their arms were made of stone as were their hearts. In reality, the paper sacrifices just created more smoke and soot.

We finished our tasks at the school several days before our departure date. This provided us with the unexpected opportunity for a quick visit across the border into China, arranged by a local travel agency.

Their arms were made of stone as were their hearts.

Lois tried to prepare us for this new and very different country. As a communist nation there were many restrictions and laws regarding Christianity and faith of which we needed to be aware. Most importantly, it was illegal for foreigners to witness to the Chinese people on the street. This was strictly enforced, but Chinese law was very confusing. Although there were restrictions, there were still active churches. Unlike Soviet Latvia where communism prohibited all church activities and expressions of faith, China offered some rights while restricting others.

In 1994 The Chinese Christian Church (CCC) operated many churches throughout the country that held regular Sunday worship services. These churches are also commonly referred to as the "Three Self Church": self-governance, self-support, and self-propagation. The word "self" meant that there was to be no outside or foreign involvement. The church operated under the direction of the Chinese government.

Pastors were trained in government-controlled seminaries. Many students were eager to share their faith within the restrictions of the CCC. Sermons were submitted to the Religious Affairs Bureau for approval, however, restricting the message. The Bureau had guidelines and often wanted sermons to focus on the good works of Jesus. The goal was to inspire good behavior in the people.

At this time there were many strictly enforced restrictions regarding worshiping and witnessing. By law, individuals were not allowed to meet together to worship at any other time or place than the scheduled Sunday morning CCC services. It was illegal to witness to children under the age of eighteen, even within the designated churches. There could be no witnessing to adults except in the church building. Bibles could only be purchased at the church. All names were recorded. These laws were strictly enforced, any offense could result in interrogations and imprisonment.

The Asian people are often shorter than I am. When in a crowd, in Macau and now in China, I found myself looking over a sea of dark hair. Just as in Haiti, our team stood out with our lighter skin tones and varying hair colors. The restrictions that Lois spoke about made me conscious of my movements. I knew we would be easy to watch. Everywhere we went curious heads turned.

Although I was grateful to trade in the shared ping pong table for a few nights of good sleep on a hotel bed, I was uneasy as I became aware that the hotel staff was tracking our movements. The elevators were slow so it seemed reasonable to use the stairways when visiting team members on separate floors. It didn't take long before someone from management told us it was forbidden to use the stairways for our "safety." That was when we all took notice that there was a desk with a hotel staff member positioned in front of the elevators on every floor. They could not track our movements if we were using the stairs.

Lois had already informed us that the rooms we stayed in were probably bugged with listening devices. We needed to be cautious of what we said, refraining from comments about communism or religion. It wasn't long before I was eager to give up my comfortable bed and return to the ping pong table and the freedoms to which I had become accustomed.

Although stressful, I was grateful for my time in China. It helped me understand the struggles of the Chinese Christians who live daily under such scrutiny. I wanted to encourage them.

Originally, when I scheduled this team, I thought we were going to be serving in Hong Kong. God then moved us to Macau. Now I wondered if God had China in mind for a future team, but what kind of team could we send, with all of the strict policies regarding religion?

Before I left for home, Lois and I discussed my returning to China with a possible prayer walking team. We were aware of an inspiring movement within the international Christian community that encouraged groups of people to travel to specific locations for the purpose of praying silently "on site with insight." Of course, prayers are heard from anywhere, but they proposed that by praying on location, those who prayed would gather special insights regarding the people and their needs, thus helping to guide their prayers.

We set a date for a prayer walking team to go to China the following year, however, no one applied to go. I was surprised and confused, but Don was not. He encouraged me to take the trip anyway and pray with Lois, knowing that wherever two or three are gathered in His name He would be there also (Matthew 18:20). In the end I was grateful that I did not have the responsibility of a team. Lois and I could focus on praying. I would also be praying that God would guide me to the people and places within this country where future MOST Ministries teams could serve.

We had several cities in mind for our prayer walking locations: Beijing, Nanjing, Xi'an and Shenyang. All were common tourist destinations. This would allow us to walk the grounds unnoticed as we silently prayed. I researched each city to understand its ancient history and current events, to help guide my thoughts and prayers. It was the summer of 1995 when I said my goodbyes to Don, this time for almost a full month.

As the plane began its descent over Beijing, I saw the magnificent city with buildings sprawling as far as the eye could see. We banked and landed in the international airport in the outlying area.

I was eager to begin "praying on site with insight." The injustices that had been endured by the Chinese Christians troubled me. They often met in secret, and these gatherings were considered the "underground church." Knowing the struggles these Christians endured fueled my desire to pray for this nation to open up to the love of Christ.

It was wonderful to serve with Lois again. We were kindred spirits, both eager to enjoy new cultures, care for others and worship God. We began our time together in prayer and Bible study. Lois was enthusiastic about a new devotional, which she provided for me: "Experiencing God," by Henry Blackaby and Claude King. As we traveled and studied together, I could understand her enthusiasm. The message was simple, *God is working everywhere in the world and He invites you to partner with Him.* As I studied Blackaby's and King's words, I hoped and prayed that one day God would lead MOST Ministries to partner with the inspiring Christians here in China.

We began our prayer walking in the city of Beijing. The huge city teemed with buses, strange-looking trucks, bicycles and rickshaws on wide roads with many lanes. I was terrified at the thought of crossing this river of movement! Lois grabbed my skirt and hung on to me as if I was a young child, dragging me into the chaotic traffic. She warned me not to stop walking; the drivers were adjusting their lanes, anticipating our forward movement. Stopping would be deadly.

God is working everywhere in the world and He invites you to partner with Him.

I was grateful when we arrived safely at the popular Tiananmen Square, a massive, open paved space before the Forbidden City designed to hold crowds of up to 600,000 people. I had seen photos of this location, some of military demonstrations with large armies marching through the square. Others were more disturbing. A young man, standing in front of a tank, defiant to death as he and other students protested during the historic Tiananmen Square Massacre of 1989.

The square was teeming with activity. Children flew colorful kites, hawkers sold trinkets, and tourists strolled everywhere. Amidst the activity I was focused on the past and praying for a future of lasting peace in this nation through Jesus. There had been many bloody battles in the history of this square, but we prayed for the blood of Jesus to cleanse this land.

To aid in my prayer time while looking like a tourist I printed Bible verses on a page that was designed to look like a tourist brochure. Not wanting my height, fair skin and red hair to draw unwanted attention, I sat on a bench and read my "brochure."

I studied and prayed the scriptures. The words of 1 Timothy 2:1-2 encouraged me to pray for China's leaders; "I urge ... that requests, prayers, intercession, and thanksgiving be made for all people—for kings and all those in authority, that we may live peaceful and quiet lives in all godliness and holiness." I longed for the Christians here to experience "quiet lives in all godliness," free to worship God as they desired.

Each day began with personal Bible study and a quiet time, seeking God's guidance. My devotions spoke about Paul's encounter with God and his miraculous conversion from persecuting Christians to becoming a devout believer. I began to pray for this to happen here in China, that those who were the persecutors would be transformed into leaders of the faith.

It was encouraging to see attendance growing in the government churches, even with all the restrictions. We attended a worship service in Beijing where we witnessed more than thirty baptisms. The large, crowded church offered multiple services. Many people sat outside listening on loud speakers. I noticed the absence of children, but rejoiced in witnessing the baptism of the adults. The crowds were a testimony to the hunger of the Chinese population for spiritual guidance.

After prayer walking in Nanjing, our next stop was Xi'an, the area known for the Terracotta Warriors, but we were not sightseeing. Our goal was to spend time with a seminary student and her family. Lois often visited the Nanjing seminary where she encouraged the students in their faith. When this student heard that Lois and I would be visiting Xi'an, she requested that Lois visit her at home, in the local commune. She was eager for Lois to meet her family.

This opportunity was a special treat for me. I had never been in a commune. It was situated in the bustling city. Although Xi'an welcomed tourists, the commune was restricted. The entrance was a gate with a guardhouse. Security guards questioned us. They wanted to know our business. Then they followed us at a distance while we walked through the maze of tall grey block apartment buildings in search of our host's fifth floor apartment.

It was a relief when the guards returned to their post, leaving us to visit and talk. The student was grateful for our visit and offered us tea and pastries. It was an honor to meet her mother who had raised her three daughters—born before the one child policy became law in 1979—to be Christians despite the harsh environment.

The mother shared her testimony. She grew up having never been to a church or hearing about Jesus. Then at the age of eighteen, God spoke to her in a dream and again at twenty-one, touching her soul and leading her on a path to discover Jesus. This was a profound experience, helping her keep her faith during the years when strong atheist influences surrounded her.

I had heard similar stories of Christ appearing in dreams; this seemed to confirm the reports that many of the Christians in closed countries begin their spiritual journey with visions or dreams of Jesus.

I was amazed and thankful that I had this opportunity to sit and talk with these women in this setting, a place where Westerners were rarely allowed. They shared openly about their life in the commune, and how the Communist Party controlled many aspects of their lives. Adults were expected to work in factories, while commune workers raised their children in nurseries. They even tracked a woman's menstrual cycle to enforce the one child policy. Officials arranged for and enforced abortions after a couple's first allotted child.

Propaganda discouraged the Chinese people from exploring the church and Christianity. It stated that Christianity was a 'new' Western religion, recently imported, therefore it was not a part of the ancient culture that is so revered by the people. The Communist Party needed to restrict Christianity as a new religion.

This conflicted with my knowledge of the Nestorian Stele, an ancient limestone block carving, which documents the existence of followers of Christ in China over 1,300 years ago. The Chinese text pays tribute to missionaries who arrived in China by 640 AD and their many followers. The author of a Christian American magazine article describing this stone tablet pleaded with his readers to pray for the Chinese countrymen that they would hear about this truth and recognize Christianity as the ancient religion it is.

I decided to see this evidence for myself. This special stele was housed in the Museum of Stele Tablets in Xi'an. After our visit with the Christian women Lois and I left to tour the museum.

It was overwhelming. There were over 3,000 stone steles offering concrete and irrefutable documentation of China's written history. Some had plaques with English descriptions, but many were not translated. I had seen the pictures of the Nestorian Stele, and knew to look for the cross, which was engraved at the top. Lois and I searched for several hours, but we could not find it. Discouraged, we stepped outside. We decided to pray.

We reentered for our final search. There it was! The evidence, carved in stone. I purchased a wax rubbing of the entire stele, five feet high and three feet wide. According to the explanation of the text, these early followers of Christ believed in the Trinity and the divinity of Jesus Christ. Christianity was not a new religion in China. It existed in the seventh century!

We could share this good news with other Christians in China, especially those in leadership positions. Out of fear, this information would not be proclaimed from the mountain tops, but could be shared in personal and private conversations, helping to refute the communist attempts to negate Christianity.

Our fourth and last destination was Shenyang, a city further east, almost to the border of China and Korea. Shenyang is a large metropolis, modern in appearance, with the usual mix of traffic that was becoming routine for me to navigate.

I was looking forward to a prearranged lunch with Martha, an American who provided medical services for Chinese children in need of specialized surgeries, like the repair of cleft palates or other disfiguring conditions. She arranged for doctors from the United States to come and perform the needed surgeries. Martha arrived at the restaurant by bicycle, the fastest mode of travel in the busy cities.

Before we began our discussions, we were offered a special tea performance. Our skilled waiter stood on the opposite side of our large round table, lifted a large metal teapot with an extra-long spout and then aimed for our cup, at least four feet away! To my astonishment the tea made a graceful arc in the air before it landed precisely in my cup; not a drop was spilled. Amazing!

Just as the tea was the perfect fit for the cup, it was soon evident that Martha would be a perfect fit as a future MOST Ministries team host. She had a genuine love for the Chinese people and desire to serve. I was relieved that at this final city, right before departure, I was able to make contact with this amazing woman. We agreed to keep in touch.

New partnerships, new insights, stronger friendships, the China prayer walking team (which had seemed so disappointing at first when no one signed up), was more amazing than I could have dreamed. I returned home rejuvenated by my extended time in prayer and committed to returning to China with more teams.

19

Abandoned

China

"In front of us was evidence that babies were dumped on the street like kittens in a sack."

These were the words of an investigator in a 1995 documentary disclosing the inhumane conditions of China's orphanages and the tragic effects of China's one child policy on infant girls. The camera focused on a bundled infant girl, recently brought to the orphanage by the local police.

The Dying Rooms, a Peabody award-winning documentary, was filmed with hidden cameras. Viewers in the Western world watched with horror as they witnessed scenes where toddlers sat in a row, arms and legs bound to their chairs. Infants lay four to a crib.

Finally, the greatest shock of all, a little girl intentionally left to die in a separate room, the dying room. After the one child policy became law, and because of the Chinese preference for boys, an alarming number of newborn girls were found abandoned on the streets. The parents presumably discarded their infant girls so they could try again to have a boy.

It was illegal to leave a child at an orphanage, so many infant girls were deserted on the city streets. This particular orphanage received an average of over thirty abandoned baby girls each month! There was an unusually high rate of death within the orphanages, caused by poor treatment, disease, and intentional neglect. Other international organizations reported similar disturbing conditions throughout China. Human Rights Watch/Asia estimates that in Shanghai during the late 1980s and early 1990s, the local orphanage's mortality rate was probably as high as 90 % (*Death by Default*, Human Rights Watch/Asia, 1996).

Even before the release of the condemning documentary, Martha, our new contact in China, was also aware of the dire needs in the orphanages. She requested that MOST Ministries bring a team to teach and encourage the overwhelmed caregivers at several local orphanages. Placed there by the government, the caregivers were frequently untrained and lacked compassion for the children.

MOST Ministries eagerly agreed and began preparations to teach the caregivers. We hoped we could break through the cultural stigma against these baby girls and help create a more humane environment.

In China it was considered an honor to give birth to a boy. It meant the gods had blessed you. The family often celebrated with fireworks, knowing their lineage would continue. Sons also provided security for parents, caring for them as they aged.

The birth of a girl was not celebrated. Girls were expected, as teens, to leave and marry into another family. With the strict restrictions of only one child per couple, the parents of infant girls now feared they would be left with no one to support them in their old age.

Girls were considered a burden even before the one child law. When a girl was born they were often named *Lai-Di* or *Zheo-Di*, meaning, "Bring a baby brother next" by the disappointed parents. According to those interviewed for *The Dying Rooms* documentary, over six million Chinese girls carried this name at the time of filming. They also stated that in the countryside girls were often referred to as "maggots in the rice."

I experienced firsthand the Chinese women's reverence for boys on my previous team. When I showed people a photo of our family, the women exclaimed that the gods must favor me because I had three sons. I explained that we also wanted a girl and how we thanked God when we finally added our daughter to our family. No one understood, so I stopped showing the photo.

The documentary also disclosed the harsh treatment of women during the pregnancy of a second child. If a woman did not submit to an abortion, then the government would take action. They might imprison the mother or even the father, until they aborted the illegal pregnancy. Women were often sterilized during the abortion process.

The one child policy was created to control China's population growth. They feared that if they continued to grow at their previous rate, the people would soon suffer. Famine would spread. When the one child policy was enacted, the government did not take into consideration the cultural desire for male children. Since the enactment it is estimated that millions of baby girls have disappeared, most due to sex selection abortions made easy by ultrasounds.

Sadly, I had been told that infanticide was also performed. It was hard to hear that baby girls were plunged into buckets of water immediately after birth before their first breath. Ironically, abandoning a baby girl on the streets was the more humane option.

The release of *The Dying Rooms* documentary had a dramatic effect on our plans. As a response to the international outcry, local Chinese orphanages were closed to foreigners. Instead, the Chinese government invited us to come and visit the elite state of the art special orphanage for gifted orphans. These children, aged seven to seventeen, were handpicked from orphanages all over China after demonstrating a special skill or ability.

Disappointed, but willing to go where God was leading, our team accepted our new destination. Our hearts continued to ache, however, over the conditions in the local orphanages. Who would help these neglected children? All we could do was hope and pray that the current negative International attention would encourage the Chinese government to make changes that would result in better care for all orphans.

Our new location was very impressive. It looked more like a college campus than an orphanage. It was evident the orphans had spent hours practicing their skills. They treated us to magnificent performances in dance, orchestra and choir. They were truly amazing. The officials encouraged us to take photos and share them with others when we returned home.

The orphanage staff consisted of well-trained teachers, not the overworked caregivers for whom we had originally prepared, but they appreciated our interactive teaching sessions. There was an immediate rapport and several interested Chinese teachers initiated conversations on faith issues. Although intentional evangelism is illegal, it is not illegal for foreigners to answer questions about Jesus or God. As a result, we were able to follow the disciple Peter's encouragement from the Bible: "Always be prepared to give an answer to everyone who asks you to give the reason for the hope you have." (1 Peter 3:15).

After our faith-filled explanations we informed the teachers about the local Chinese Christian Church and the inspiring pastor who preached the truths of Christ, as well as he could, under the demands of the government. We had been fortunate to hear his sermons earlier that week. His growing church served 2,000 members during multiple services and through TV monitors in a courtyard. We hoped the curious teachers would continue to ask questions of local Christians long after we left.

It was challenging to understand the religious community in China. On one hand, Sunday mornings felt normal. Many of the official Chinese churches were overflowing, and led by strong believing men. Bibles could be purchased at the church and the worship experience was similar to my home church.

We also experienced firsthand, however, how the government created the illusion of religious freedom. Although it was legal to purchase a Bible, it could only be bought at a church, where the transaction was then registered. Many feared placing their names on the registry, never knowing if the tide would swing even more strongly against Christianity.

The people were far from free. Laws and rules abounded to restrict common Christian practices, like gathering together to study or pray, as the Communist Party desperately attempted to control the spread of Christianity.

Thankfully, their attempts were failing. The Holy Spirit was clearly at work, opening the hearts and minds of the people. I thanked God for His ultimate wisdom in redirecting our team and allowing us to share our faith with the teachers of the orphanage.

Our plans for serving the young children in China's orphanages did not turn out as we expected, so we turned our vision to the other end of life's spectrum—China's elderly and dying.

Before I returned to the States, Martha and I discussed the possibility of a China hospice team. Her ministry worked closely with the local medical administrators, making it possible for her to explore their interest in learning about this unique philosophy. As a result of her discussions with hospitals in Beijing and Shenyang, there were invitations extended to MOST Ministries for a hospice training team. Steve, who had led many teams, agreed to lead this first China hospice team in August of 1996 since I was unavailable. Eileen and I were busy moving out of my home and into the office at Concordia College.

When the team returned, I was amazed to hear that in just two weeks they had presented to over a thousand physicians, nurses, social workers and caregivers, and was even more amazed when Steve told me that at one facility, they witnessed to thirty-two physicians and nurses who received Jesus Christ as their personal Savior! They asked the right questions, and our team responded.

The hospice curriculum helped to guide the discussions. The participants' eagerness to learn about Christ was the result of seeds that had been sown by a previous ministry, independent of MOST Ministries. Our team was fortunate enough to witness the blessing of the harvest.

The overall response by the medical community to the hospice philosophy was less encouraging. Steve shared that the participants were engaged and interested as the team presented on long-term care for the chronically ill and elderly, but they appeared uncomfortable and disengaged when the team discussed compassionate care for the terminally ill. They struggled with discussions regarding death and dying.

I wondered why. Could it be that as a communist country, the medical community held the same views as communist Latvia? Were they abandoning people when they were of no use to society? I decided it would be necessary for me to learn more about the culture before considering another hospice team.

Over the next two years as I led teams to Ghana, Haiti, Mexico, Latvia and Cote d'Ivoire, I couldn't stop thinking about China. Deep down I knew that God wanted me to go back.

After prayer and discussion, it was decided that Lois and I would spend time prayer walking on the campuses of universities and seminaries in Shanghai, Nanjing and Wuhan. We would also seek out professionals who might be willing to discuss the topic of the Chinese culture and their attitudes towards death and dying, but we were not exactly sure how we would meet these individuals.

It was unusual for me to plan a trip with unresolved variables. I tried to trust that God would arrange for us to find the right individuals to talk to, but I still had doubts, wishing that we had been able to prearrange more meetings.

It was April of 1998 when I departed. Throughout my visit God did guide me to many people who were willing to talk. In Wuhan there was a mix up in our hotel arrangements that almost left Lois and me with no lodging. Eventually, we ended up at the apartment of the director of the seminary where we had hoped to pray the next day. We explained our housing predicament. Through her family's efforts they found us another hotel. While assisting us, they asked, "Why are you in Wuhan?" We explained our mission to pray for the area, including the seminary and our hope to also meet with professionals to discuss the hospice philosophy.

As I explained my desire to bring hospice care to China, the director, a strong Christian woman, listened intently. After a thoughtful pause, she smiled and declared, "I know why there was confusion over your housing, which allowed us to meet. God has sent you to me. I have been praying about the elderly in the new Elder Care Home that I have recently established. I have been asking God for wisdom and guidance in their physical and spiritual care, knowing death will eventually come." Then with the sound and look of pure amazement, she stated. "I am shocked that God answered my prayers by sending you all the way from America!"

The director also introduced me to a professor of sociology and philosophy at one of the largest universities. We had an opportunity to talk about the Chinese culture and hospice care, as well as our own faith as we walked outside for several hours. He was a Christian, and explained that being out in the open was the safest way to speak about faith issues. It was a sobering reminder of the caution we needed to practice.

"I am shocked that God answered my prayers by sending you all the way from America!"

He was skeptical about the Chinese culture being ready for such radical medical care as the hospice philosophy. The Chinese people, he told me, were reluctant to even discuss death, let alone embrace a teaching centered on the care of the dying.

The more he understood the humane and loving practice of hospice care, however, the more he wished to see his countrymen cared for in this fashion. He believed that the current medical community did not offer good care to the terminally ill. As we walked and talked, he changed his mind, and encouraged me to bring hospice care to China. Although it was counter to the culture, he knew the people would benefit greatly. He hoped and prayed there would be doctors and nurses who would be ready to embrace this compassionate care.

In the end I felt that if MOST Ministries was asked to return with a team that God was leading me to accept the invitation. I also knew that since spiritual teachings were a part of the hospice philosophy, we would be allowed to share the basics of our faith, as the previous team had. It would be a rare opportunity to enter China with permission to speak on faith issues.

Shortly after I returned home, one of the contacts in Beijing did officially invite MOST Ministries to introduce the hospice philosophy to the medical staff and administrators of a government-run hospital. We accepted. Several of our past hospice team members, including

Dr. Sosars and Rev. Jasper, were enthusiastic about the opportunity to present their teachings in China.

A year later, in April 1999, I returned with a hospice training team. As our team members discussed hospice's compassionate attitude towards dying patients we were discouraged by the Chinese doctors who demonstrated a lack of concern for the dying. They were always trying to re-focus our seminars away from hospice care and back to long-term care for the elderly.

I was frustrated at how uncomfortable the doctors and nurses were with the topic of death. I wondered, *why is this so difficult?*

As our seminar progressed, we learned of several common cultural practices that were hindering our progress. In China a doctor's honor was at stake if he could not cure his patient. To admit openly to a patient that they were dying was unthinkable; it would harm the doctor's reputation. As a result, patients were rarely told of terminal illnesses! This made it impossible for the patient or their families to prepare for death, a philosophy the exact opposite of hospice care.

I had not imagined that the first challenge in China would be to help these doctors overcome their reluctance in sharing the diagnosis of a terminal illness. We desperately tried to stress the importance of informing and then supporting the patient and family during this difficult time, but our words seemed to fall on deaf ears.

How different from Dr. Sosars' and his Latvian staff who desired to walk alongside the terminally ill patients, offering them the best care they could provide. It was difficult for me to understand this culture with attitudes so foreign from my own.

It was disturbing to learn that hospitals, also concerned about their reputations, discharged patients when they were about to die. They wanted to avoid poor statistics. It seemed impossible to teach the idea of compassionately caring for the dying in a culture where the professionals, who were supposed to help, were conditioned to ignore and abandon.

I was frustrated and disappointed when I returned home, but I was not ready to give up. China was a very large nation; I hoped there would be a region progressive enough to hear our message and receive it.

The next year we accepted an invitation from medical professionals in Dalian, a modern city on the Eastern seacoast. Our host was hopeful that this area would be different, more open-minded. We also agreed to present at the Wuhan seminary, knowing they were eager for our teachings. Many of the same team members were ready to return for one more try.

Unfortunately, the medical professionals in Dalian were no different. After three teams went to three different regions, the results were still discouraging.

However, it was here, on our third China hospice trip, that we finally received the insight we needed. A Chinese man bravely shared with me the Chinese people's most feared superstition regarding death. There was a sincere belief that speaking about death would result in personal tragedy; someone they loved would die. I sensed the fear in the young man. He clearly felt that he was putting his loved ones at risk just to tell me this. He admitted he would like to discuss the topic further, but fear prevented him.

Now I understood the tensions from the participants as they disengaged or redirected our discussions. They feared that their participation would bring tragedy into their lives! No wonder it had been so difficult to introduce hospice care. Not only were the participants reluctant to share a diagnosis, they genuinely feared publicly discussing the topic.

At last, I understood and felt compassion for them! Unfortunately, there would be no special hospital beds to provide hospice care for the dying in China. Knowing we could not change the culture, our Christian hosts and I agreed we would not accept any more requests for hospice training teams to China until the culture was ready. All we could do was pray that we had planted seeds through our presentations that might mature when this society was ready to allow for their growth.

There was one ray of hope for our weary team at our last location, the seminary in Wuhan. In stark contrast to the government run hospital staff, the director and her students were eager to learn and discuss end-of-life issues and sensitive care for the dying. Their Christian faith allowed them to disregard the common superstitions. These students were enthusiastic about learning how to help those who would someday be in their spiritual care.

At the end of our time together, one student wrote this encouraging note, sharing his special insight on the spiritual care offered by Christians as we lovingly care for the dying and his promise to share this message:

> *You midwife a dying person to heaven, because you bring heaven onto this world and into the heart of that person. In the darkest time you shine for him, in the deepest despair you bring hope to him... You have taught us a lesson, not only on end of life care, but also on how to be a Christian. The feet are many in China but the hands ready to wash are few. It's our glory to receive this love bonfire from you... though we Christians are few in China we will try to bring this idea into reality as early as possible.*

20

Let Your Light Shine Before Men

China

"Welcome to Kunming, China," said the local Religious Affairs Director as he greeted our team at our hotel. He grasped my hand for a firm handshake and then made a slight bow. "For your protection I will be accompanying you at each of your eyeglass clinic sites."

I thanked him, but was not reassured by his declaration. I knew it was also his job to watch over our team and report any infractions of China's many laws, especially regarding witnessing. Our team understood the severe restrictions and penalties. We would not be sharing our faith during our clinics. We prayed that our loving acts of service would speak the words of faith that our lips could not.

It was 2004, four years after my final China Hospice team. I had returned to China with an eyeglass team that I knew would be well-received. With the local government's permission, the Concordia Welfare director invited our MOST Ministries team to serve several villages outside the large city of Kunming with free eyeglasses.

When we arrived in this large and modern city, I was surprised to see that China was changing and beginning to look more like Western nations. Large colorful billboards advertising products were a new and unusual sight. It was evidence that capitalism was entering this communist country. However, some things had not changed. We still could not speak freely. We honored China's laws and never once shared our faith. The director was true to his word and kept us safe in the many crowded cities. He even shut one site down when the people became unruly. We appreciated his assistance.

As the end of our time in China drew near, the local government officials arranged a dinner in our honor. They thanked us for our service and the genuine care we offered to their countrymen. As the evening drew to an end, the Religious Affairs Director surprised us by approaching our Christian host and making an incredible offer. He said, "You and the team have treated our people with such respect and dignity. What can we do to show our gratitude?"

Our host was shocked. Thinking quickly, he said "There are fifteen people in your province who are Christians. They would like permission to build a church." Without delay, permission was granted!

It was overwhelming. A church was to be built as a result of our team and we had not even shared our faith! I remembered my earlier prayers for China, in which I pleaded with God to reveal Himself miraculously to His people by changing the hearts of the Chinese officials. Now, several years later God had used our team to soften the heart of a leader, allowing for a church. It was almost beyond belief.

> A church was to be built as a result of our team. And we had not even shared our faith!

I was a bit skeptical. Would the man keep his word and allow for this church to be built? I hoped and prayed that his words were more than just an empty promise.

The following year I returned to Kunming, China to lead an English as a Second Language (ESL) team. We would serve the tenth graders at Zhan Yi Yu School, a total of 700 students! The immense population and numbers in China continue to amaze me.

These students had been studying English but had never heard it spoken by native English speakers. We were to hold classes and engage the students in English conversations. As part of our curriculum, we planned to discuss common holidays observed in America, like

Christmas, Easter and Thanksgiving. This would allow our team to share the Biblical beliefs of the many Westerners who celebrate these special days.

Our first full day in China was a Sunday. Our host brought us early to the local Christian church, guaranteeing us a seat indoors where we could be out of the cold. He knew that the crowds would soon gather and fill this little church, inside and out.

The service began with hymns. I listened as tunes that were familiar to me were sung with new tonal sounds. I sang along in my mind, but found that I could only remember one or two of the verses. I was impressed as these Chinese Christians sang with passion and conviction—all of the verses of the hymns—from memory. I was told that our North American habit of selecting just a few verses, often to save time, is confusing to them because each hymn tells a story. To skip a verse is like omitting some of the story.

We enjoyed our visit. The pastor clearly loved the Lord, and his parishioners were very welcoming. After the service they enjoyed requesting and posing for photos with us Americans, a common activity. Americans are a rare sight, so pictures with their "new American friends" are often treasured.

After several days of ESL classes, I was invited back to meet with this pastor. We met at his small shop where he sold ice cream bars and food items to support himself. We sat by a warming stove where, with the help of an interpreter, he explained that for several years he had been asking the Religious Affairs Bureau for permission to expand his church facilities. His request was always denied. The Bureau, he said, feared he was the leader of a cult. "After you Westerners chose to worship at my church, they recognized and acknowledged Christianity as a true religion." He told me, "They have now granted us permission to expand! It is truly a miracle!"

He went on to tell how God was working mightily in this region and that he had recently attended the dedication of a newly constructed church. He shared how this new church was built because of an eyeglass team from the United States that had come to the city the year before.

The church, promised to the previous year's team, was *already* built and dedicated! My heart sang for joy as I shared with this pastor that I had been the leader of that team.

We both sat, overwhelmed, as we contemplated these miracles. In both situations the team planted invisible seeds and God brought forth the harvest. What a joy it was to pray with the pastor, his wife and young son. We thanked God for His mercy and the miracles resulting from the team's silent witness in a country closed to foreign witnessing.

God used us to do His work, just as it is proclaimed in the passage from Matthew 5:16: "Let your light shine before men, that they may see your good works, and glorify your Father which is in Heaven."

Indonesia

21

Stained Glass Windows

Indonesia

Traffic whizzed by at incredible speeds. Expressways were stacked four to five levels deep and intertwined with tall skyscrapers. It took my breath away. I was a big city girl, but this made Chicago look like a small town. Jakarta, Indonesia, a city of nine million people, had me wide-eyed and riveted to my seat.

We were safely delivered to a luxurious home in a wealthy suburb. This would be the lodging for our eyeglass team. From there, we would set out each day to eight different sites. This home seemed too extravagant when I considered the living conditions of those whom we were there to serve. As I crawled into bed after a grueling 34 hours of travel, however, I thanked the Lord for such wonderful accommodations.

It was the year 2000 and this was MOST Ministries' first team to Indonesia, a nation comprised of 17,000 islands. The city of Jakarta is on the Island of Java. Jakarta has the highest population and also a great deal of wealth; however, as with many large cities, there are pockets of urban poverty. We were there to serve those individuals, holding clinics to provide for those who could not afford eyeglasses.

Indonesia is predominantly Muslim, so we relied on our hosts to advise us regarding the sharing of our faith. Many Muslims take great offense when Christians speak of Jesus' death and resurrection. Although they believe that Jesus was a great prophet, they do not believe that Jesus died on the cross. They do not understand the new life offered through faith in His resurrection.

The Christian Broadcasting Network (CBN) who sponsored our first three sites surprised us by encouraging us to have a strong Christian presence through witnessing and prayer. I was amazed that many of those who went through the testing and fitting process for eyeglasses were also eager to wait for our Christian prayers. Pa Budhi, our host for this clinic, formed small groups where he led conversations, asked for prayer concerns, and then had the participants pray for each other.

One businessman asked for prayer for his constant stomach pain. He was miserable. He had tried everything he could, beseeching his gods for relief for over thirty days. Pa Budhi shared his faith with him, and then gave him the *Help From Above* scripture booklet in his language.

The very next day the businessman returned to the clinic with a smile. His pain was gone. "Who is this God who heals?" He asked Pa Budhi. He was eager to learn more.

Missionaries from the United States sponsored our next few eyeglass clinics. They had established a relationship with several impoverished communities within the city.

One of the sites was in a predominately Muslim area that had strong opposition to outside influence. The village elders would allow our clinic, but prohibited witnessing. We agreed to their terms.

When we arrived, we saw that this was a densely packed community. It would be impossible to drive our large bus with all of our equipment to our clinic site in the center of the village. Having no other choice, we parked on the outskirts and hoisted the ten heavy duffle bags of eyeglasses and vision equipment onto our backs. We walked the narrow path toward our clinic site, the home of a believer.

The community elders approached and stood along the path, wary of our presence and watching suspiciously as we passed. I sensed hostility and knew we would be carefully watched.

As we made our way, I was surprised to see a Christian church with boarded-up windows. I wondered if this meant that the church was no longer in use. I discovered it was an active church, served by the local missionaries. The stained-glass windows depicting Jesus were offensive to the Muslims so they had been told to cover them.

There was excitement about our presence. People stood on porches, looked out of windows, and leaned over balconies to get a good view of us. Everywhere we looked, residents were gathered at a respectful distance, watching us.

There were many challenges in setting up the clinic in the small two-story home. We were a large team with twenty members, including the interpreters. I wondered where we would find enough space for the testing and distribution of the eyeglasses. At first glance it seemed impossible!

People lined up to register. Everywhere I looked there was a sea of people waiting for the next step in their testing process. Somehow, we managed to keep order.

Occasionally, I spoke with the women in the waiting area. They were so appreciative of our help! Through an interpreter, they expressed their thanks. Although I shook hands with the women, I knew not to expect a handshake from a man; that would be culturally inappropriate. There were no outwardly demonstrative hugs or tears of joy as in other cultures, but their smiles, as they left wearing their new glasses, said it all.

It was a hot, crowded, and stressful day. As the clinic came to a close, we packed up our equipment. The men hoisted the duffel bags on their shoulders and we returned to the bus.

Once again, the elders were lined up along the path, but this time they were smiling and cheering along with the residents of the community, as we passed by. The hostility I had felt as we entered the area had disappeared and the air was now festive, filled with gratefulness for our efforts. We also noted that most of the elders were wearing our glasses.

As a result of our visit, the boarded-up church was allowed to let their stained glass windows be visible. The residents could see the images of Jesus and sunlight could shine again into this small church. The Imam, the Muslim leader of the community, also declared that anyone wanting to attend that church could do so without penalties.

I marveled at how God so often worked through our silent witness, softening hearts as only He could do.

India

22

We Will Act in Faith

India

All traffic came to a stop. I peered out of the bus window to see the problem. It was a cow, lounging on the road. This was not the typical North American black and white dairy cow. This cow was gray with horns that were painted bright colors.

In India cows are sacred, and allowed to freely roam. It's illegal to injure or kill one. No one made an attempt to move her. Instead, we waited. Finally, the traffic formed a new lane around the cow. She laid in the road, lazily watching as we drove by.

Some in India consider the cow the "mother" of all civilization, due to her life-giving milk. It's believed that feeding a snack of bread or fruit to a roaming cow will bring good luck.

India was new and exciting to me. I loved the bright colored clothing of the women. Many wore beautiful saris, a dress made of seven yards of uniquely-designed silk wrapped around the body. Each woman was like a walking piece of art.

It was the year 2000, and my team members and I had just finished a MOST Ministries Vacation Bible School team for several Christian orphanages in South India run by the ministry Bethania Kids. As the team's time together came to an end, most of the members headed home. One member, Dot, and I embarked on another mission. We traveled hundreds of miles north to the city of Ambur. There we met with Dr. Joel, the director of Bethesda Hospital, to explain the basics of hospice care.

Dot was enthusiastic about our mission. Many months earlier she had introduced me to Bethesda hospital's chaplain, Rev. Udhayanesan, who was visiting the United States for further training. He was passionate about hospice care and wished to introduce it to Bethesda Hospital. He encouraged Dot and me to arrange this meeting with Dr. Joel, hoping it would result in MOST Ministries receiving an invitation to return with a future hospice training team.

Rev. Udhayanesan had spoken highly of this Christian hospital, describing it as a beacon of light in a Hindu community, and having an exceptional medical reputation. I could hardly wait to see for myself.

It had an interesting history. In the early 1900s, a missionary doctor from the United States served the area, using an ox-drawn cart as a mobile clinic. He traveled to remote villages, up to twenty miles away. As needs increased, he requested a hospital. In 1921, a modest 16-bed hospital was built. The name Bethesda was chosen for the Hebrew meaning of the word, "House of Mercy," and to commemorate the biblical recounting of the healing waters at the pool of Bethesda. Over the years, as Bethesda Hospital grew, it continued to live up to its name, offering mercy and healing to all who entered—even those who could not pay.

Our van pulled into the expansive hospital grounds, and Dr. Joel warmly greeted us. The grounds were spacious, tree-filled, and peaceful—a stark contrast to the overpopulated and crowded villages I had seen during my travels throughout India. The hospital was a complex of several small buildings, with an open-air waiting room (a common style in warmer climates, where airflow is important).

As Dr. Joel toured us around the grounds, we could see it was a perfect place to find peace, rest, and good health. Patients could be seen visiting outside in small groups with families or strolling the campus. Monkeys provided entertainment as they swung from the treetops.

We stopped in front of the chapel, a unique building designed to reflect the early Christian symbol of the fish. The roof arched as the back of a fish while one side supported a tall cement tail-like structure engraved with a cross. It, too, was an open-air building.

Near the front of the grounds sat an old trailer that had once been used for the hospital's mobile clinics. It was a reminder of their humble beginnings and the hospital's continuing desire to go into the community and serve. Dr. Joel and his staff continued this tradition by traveling on weekends to rural villages, providing free medical care for those who could not make it into the city for treatment. Many were AIDS (Acquired Immunodeficiency Syndrome) victims.

Dr. Joel, the business manager, and the department heads met with the two of us to hear about hospice care. It was an intense and emotional meeting. They listened intently as I explained the multi-disciplined approach. Their questions and discussions reassured me that, unlike China, they were ready to embrace this new philosophy.

However, finances were tight. Could they manage the added expenses of a new program? Currently there were no extra beds or rooms to dedicate to hospice care. Much of the discussion focused on finances. How could they serve the poor with their limited budget? We prayed together.

All eyes were on Dr. Joel, whose head was bowed. Eventually, he lifted his head and spoke. "We cannot afford such a program," he admitted. Then with passion and reverence he said, "but Christ commands us to serve the dying. We will act in faith." They knew it would be difficult, but trusted that God would provide.

It was decided. MOST Ministries would return with a hospice training team. Rev. Udhayanesan was pleased.

After the meeting with Dr. Joel and his staff, I had the opportunity to meet with forty pastors from the Ambur District who listened while I explained the role of the chaplain in hospice care. They were eager for our training. They spoke with passionate concern regarding the growing number of AIDS victims in their communities.

...Christ commands us to serve the dying. We will act in faith.

It broke my heart to listen to their stories of ministering to those wasting away from this dreadful disease. They longed for help and encouragement.

Back home I didn't hesitate to contact Dr. Vilnis Sosars, who said "yes" to yet another country. It had been six years since this compassionate Latvian doctor first spoke to me regarding hospice care. Since then MOST Ministries had sent out seven different hospice training teams and reached out to three different countries. Dr. Sosars accompanied us to each new country, willingly offering his continued support to those who were interested.

Each country's customs and beliefs impacted how we presented the material. It also affected their ability to receive it. As I began helping the team with the preparations for creating hospice materials for India, I wondered: *what were their cultural beliefs regarding death?*

The greater Indian population practices Hinduism, a belief in reincarnation: a repetitive cycle of life and death. Many believe that after death, each soul visits heaven briefly, then returns to earth and begins the life cycle again. The soul's new form will be determined by its past life. If they pleased the gods through the appropriate rituals, meditation and sacrifices they will return as a higher form, progressing from insect, to animal to human. Within the human race, they will be born into the level of caste, or class, they have achieved.

The caste system in India is a ranking of the population, with four specific castes. It is similar to our North American concept of lower, middle and higher-class citizens. In India, however, your caste is permanent. It is based on your family of origin, not your income or job. A lower caste citizen must remain a lower class citizen; there is no hope of change until the next life. The lowest are simply called the "untouchables." This is the population that Mother Theresa so faithfully served.

Many Hindus believe that each person has earned the current life they have been given. The lower caste citizens and untouchables, therefore, deserve to be where they are because they did not please the gods in their past lives. This belief has resulted in a lack of compassion among the wealthier castes for the poorer and lower castes.

I was glad we would be teaching in a Christian hospital to a staff where Christ's model of love and compassion for every human being, no matter what caste, was practiced.

As we prepared for this team, Dot and several other team members requested that we also provide encouragement to the women of India. They understood that the Indian women were often considered of lesser value, the lowliest within their castes. It was only those women in the highest castes that were encouraged to study and allowed opportunities at higher education. The team members longed to encourage all the Indian women, no matter their caste, reassuring them of their great value in God's eyes. It was determined to make this a dual focused team: hospice training and women's ministry.

A special three-day women's Bible study was prepared for the women on staff with Bethesda Hospital and others in the area. The team members also planned to support and encourage the wives of the forty pastors while their husbands attended the hospice chaplaincy training sessions.

After much preparation our MOST Ministries team arrived in November 2002. Our time began with a worship service and special welcoming ceremony in the unique fish-shaped chapel. After inspiring speeches by our hosts, each team member was presented with a traditional garland made of flowers, sandalwood nuts, and gold-foiled papers. In addition, we were also "shawled" with a brightly woven shawl placed over our shoulders. It was a very special and warm Indian-style welcome.

The women's Bible study was well received. Over forty women attended and listened intently to the many examples of God's love and care for women. Participants were each presented a Bible in the local language of Tamil to continue exploring God's deep love for them.

The pastor's wives appreciated our attention to their needs. We encouraged them and provided a safe haven for them to share their common struggles. In an effort to support the wives, our social worker also met with the pastors. Our insightful team members understood that to truly help the Indian women, they needed to speak to the men. The social worker encouraged the pastors to fight against the common cultural devaluing of women, especially within their marriages by reminding them of Christ's command: "Husbands, love your wives, just as Christ loved the church and gave himself up for her." (Ephesians 5:25)

After the Scriptures were read, one of the pastors, a recent widower, stood before his peers and confessed that he had not loved or honored his wife as he should have. He implored his peers to reject the social norms against women and to love their wives as Christ commands. "I did not value and love my wife as I should have, and for me, it is too late." Hearing the widower's plea was moving. His emotional pain was palpable. I hoped the pastors would heed his words and treasure their precious wives.

Across the hospital campus, Dr. Joel and his staff listened while Dr. Sosars and others discussed the multidisciplinary approach of hospice care. I quietly took a seat in the back. Although I had heard these lectures many times, this time was different. Never before had our presenters had the opportunity to speak openly and directly to a medical community who already believed in Christ. I was mesmerized and inspired as I heard the teachings anew. The presenters shared from their hearts knowing they were speaking to many who already understood Christ's call to serve. The doctors and nurses listened intently, eager to begin this new program.

Prior to the team's arrival, Dr. Joel managed to set aside three beds as a special unit for hospice care. It was not much, just three simple beds lying side by side with barely enough room for family members to gather around. But it was a start.

On our final day, the team, Dr. Joel, Rev. Udhayanesan and several hospital staff gathered to participate in the official dedication of

Bethesda Hospital's first hospice ward. Rev. Udhayanesan was very pleased.

Secure in the knowledge that the hospital staff and the local pastors would do their best to answer Christ's call to offer compassionate care to the dying, I left India feeling encouraged.

One year later, in 2003, I was in India with an eyeglass team, invited by Dr. Joel to serve the poor in the local community. I was eager to visit the hospital and see their new hospice ward, which I heard had been moved and recently refurbished. I was pleasantly surprised to see that it was now three well-appointed private rooms, each with its own bathroom. *Why did the hospital invest so much into these rooms?* I wondered. *Weren't they on a tight budget?*

Dr. Joel explained their strategy for funding the new hospice ward. Bethesda Hospital had a reputation for being one of the finest hospitals in the area, but it lacked the nicer amenities, causing wealthy patients to go elsewhere. These updated private rooms changed that. When they were not serving hospice patients, these rooms were made available to wealthy patients who required only a short stay. Many were willing to pay extra for the private rooms when recovering from surgeries. The income raised during these short stays covered the costs to run the whole hospice program which provided for the many poor terminally ill patients who could not otherwise afford such comfortable care.

One of the staff was eager to tell me about her beloved aunt who had been a patient in this hospice ward. With tears in her eyes she told me of how her aunt, a poor retired teacher, received loving care. She died with dignity.

As I walked the refurbished hospice ward, I looked in on a teen-age girl who was dying of AIDS. Her mother sat beside her, tenderly stroking her hair and holding her hand. I wanted to console her, but we spoke different languages. As I stood there quietly, I hoped the mother could sense my sorrow.

It was comforting to know that the doctors and nurses would be keeping the young girl comfortable and that the mother could count on a trained social worker and chaplain to help her during this difficult time.

While striving to help Bethesda hospital develop their hospice program, I was also moved to help them serve their smallest patients, premature infants. Bethesda was a "Baby Friendly Hospital," a prestigious ranking in India, but it was still limited and lacked specialized equipment.

"We do not have blood pressure cuffs small enough, or special preemie incubators." Dr. Charlottee Manoharan, the director of pediatrics, said. A flicker of deep sadness crossed her face. I wondered how many little lives had been lost due to this lack of specialized equipment.

Her words and expressions played over and over in my mind, long after I returned home. Could Don and I help? With so many needs worldwide, we have to guard our hearts. We cannot give money to all who are in need, but this seemed different. I could not stop thinking about her desire to care for these fragile new lives.

After speaking to Don, we prayed and approached our church. Would they consider raising money to help purchase this needed equipment?

Our church's mission committee fully embraced the cause. Within months I contacted Dr. Joel—our church had raised $14,000! They were overwhelmed.

With exchange rates in their favor, and the low costs to build, this money opened new possibilities for this department. After much prayer, they decided to build a new pediatric ICU building, a dream of Dr. Manoharan's.

In 2009 I attended the dedication of the new building. I remembered attending my first dedication at this hospital, a small ward of three beds to serve the terminally ill with hospice care. Now I was about to participate in the dedication of a whole new specialized pediatric building!

I was asked to speak as a special guest. I felt humble and small as I considered my limited role in this project. I had simply been the messenger, bringing a request to my home church for life saving equipment. It was God who inspired the generosity of our church members and led the vision of the hospital staff. In my smallness I was aware of God's greatness. All I could do was give Him the glory.

In my smallness I was aware of God's greatness.

After the ceremony we went to the new building, with its gleaming white exterior, for the official ribbon cutting. To the left of the door was a large plaque commemorating this dedication to the "Glory of God." After the mention of St. Luke Church, it stated "Opened by Ms. Gayle Sommerfeld, USA."

As I cut the ribbon and the two ends fell to the ground, I considered the precious new lives that could be given the care that they deserved, all because the Lord opened the hearts of many in response to a need.

23

A Hope and a Future

India

"Can I please have a minute of your time?"

The request came from Jabus, the headmaster of the Concordia Higher Education School in Ambur, India. In 2003, Bethesda Hospital had asked MOST Ministries to return after our hospice training and women's ministry team to offer a Christian marriage retreat for its staff. Don and I had just finished the last presentation of our MOST Ministries marriage seminar, and I assumed Jabus' request was in response to the marriage presentations.

Jabus seemed distraught. What had we said? I drew up a chair and invited him to join me. However, his concerns were not about his marriage. Tears formed in his eyes as he began to discuss the ever-increasing rate of suicides among his more than 2,000 students.

I was glad I was sitting down as I listened to his explanation of the pressures in India that make children feel so hopeless. "Newspapers publish all the scores for the National Examination," he said. "The community can see whether a child has passed or failed." This national test is given in the second grade and again when entering secondary school.

For students who fail, having their failure publicized to the community brings intense shame to themselves and their families. In a culture where honor is the greatest achievement, to be shamed publicly is devastating. I wondered how these young children could be expected to bear this burden of public failure! Feeling shamed, these desperate students chose suicide as their apology believing it was the only way to restore their families' honor.

Jabus shared with me the most recent suicide, an eight-year-old second-grade girl who took her life because she failed the examination. I hardly knew how to respond, except to add my tears to his. I knew God was calling MOST Ministries to help him reach out to his students.

As we explored ways to address the suicides, I asked him if his school had any counselors or social workers. "No," he said. "There is no one to help guide the children through stressful situations."

After discussing many ideas, it appeared that the first steps in helping with suicide prevention would be to train teachers to recognize the early signs of depression. Then we would equip them with the basic skills needed to counsel those students.

I committed to returning with a team that could train his teachers with the necessary counseling skills. Once home, I began the process of recruiting a team. Even with all of my past experiences of watching God provide, I still marveled as He led me to Linda. She had recently been named the "School Counselor of the Year" in the state of Oregon. Through her efforts a psychologist, Murl, and schoolteacher also joined our team. With the addition of two more professionals, all from the Portland area, plus Aruna, a nurse who grew up in the Ambur area, we felt confident we could prepare materials for a summer seminar in 2005.

While this team of professionals was busy preparing their lectures on suicide prevention, I was off to India again, leading an eyeglass team. During our flight, one of my team members, Dot, struck up a conversation with her seatmate. He turned out to be an official of the Church of South India (CSI). Dot invited me into their conversation and soon I was sharing with this official my new concerns about child and adolescent suicide in India.

He admitted that it was also a problem for the large number of students within his CSI schools. It wasn't long before I invited him to send twenty of his teachers to Ambur for our future suicide prevention seminar.

When I returned to the United States after the eyeglass team's work, I focused my research on the Indian culture. What was causing the children to lose hope? I contacted a seasoned missionary, Herb Hoefer. He had served the India Evangelical Lutheran Church for fifteen years in Ambur. Herb shared that he was aware of some children who were so distraught after the tests, fearing that they failed, that they took their life even before the results were posted! Some, he said, if they had only waited, would have learned that they had passed.

Herb said he had spent many years encouraging the children, telling them that with Jesus there are no castes. All are precious in His sight. He was grateful that MOST Ministries would also share this message.

We also discussed the incredible pressures on the young girls and women who struggle in a male-dominated culture. Herb told me "Eve teasing" was another cause of suicide and depression among women and girls. Eve teasing occurs when a boy, or group of boys, harasses a girl. It could be as simple as publicly calling out their name as she passes by. Even if the girl did nothing to intentionally attract the boy's attention, culturally the blame for the shameful actions of the boy is placed on the girl, who is assumed to have enticed him. Since it is through the perceived innocence of a young woman that she achieves honor in her community, she may be punished by her parents for being provocative (they assume) and tainting the family name. Nothing happens to the boys. They are considered innocent, "just boys being boys."

The young girl and her parents may feel disgraced, believing that since she had been singled out publicly in their community in this shameful way, her reputation is forever marred. They might even fear that this disgrace could negatively affect any future arranged marriages! This is a young girl's only hope for her future. Some girls are so distraught and hopeless over the shame, they commit suicide.

Herb also shared some of the impacts of the culturally accepted marriage dowry system, the arranged gift the bride's parents pay to the husband and his family for marrying her. I was surprised to learn that a husband and his parents may request additional dowry payments from the wife and daughter-in-law years after the wedding. This creates a great strain on the wife, who has little to no power in the marriage.

Women who cannot pay the continued dowry, or who feel trapped and helpless, may resort to suicide. It's a common enough practice to have a name: "dowry death." Some women will commit suicide rather than saddle their parents with the burden of financial distress. My heart ached as my eyes were opened to the plight of these women.

On one of my previous visits to India I had heard of five sisters who committed suicide together as a gift to their father. He had worried about the many dowries he would need to pay and had often said, "What have I done that the gods have punished me with five daughters?" The sisters decided to relieve their father of his burden.

The more I learned from Herb, the more I urgently desired to share Jesus' love in India. At our request, Jabus had sent us twenty-five case histories of student suicides. They were filled with heart wrenching scenarios, like a young girl who took her life after feeling her teacher had embarrassed her in front of the class. We hoped to use these scenarios as teaching tools in our seminars. Could anything have been done differently? Had there been signs of depression?

After months of preparation, we arrived in Ambur with an array of teaching materials. This included a 200-page syllabus for all the teachers attending, a scripture resource index of over forty topics organized alphabetically from "Anger" to "Wisdom," and additional materials for a one-day presentation to the forty local pastors and their wives.

Twenty CSI teachers attended, traveling a day's journey from Chennai. Twenty-five teachers from the five local schools in Ambur participated, as well as several schoolteachers and administrators from other districts. Our attendees could potentially affect more than 20,000 students.

Our seminar presentations incorporated interactive lectures as well as small group and panel discussions. Kalavathy, a middle-aged teacher of English and Social Studies at Jabus' school, stood out among her peers. She eagerly volunteered for role-playing opportunities and contributed insight to the discussions. She had such presence! I sought her out during the breaks. Kalavathy was a compassionate woman who demonstrated deep love and concern for her students. She provided used clothing for her students who were desperately poor and helped raise money for their school supplies. Kalavathy also faithfully prayed with her students. We quickly became friends.

The seminar moved along quickly as the facts about suicide were presented and common myths exposed. We tried to dispel the common myth that asking a person if they are considering suicide will influence them to do so. The fact is, having a conversation will not plant the idea, and for those who have considered it, the conversation could be lifesaving.

We were awed at seeing the transformation of the brain from over-activity to being peaceful in prayer.

The presenters were engaging. The psychologist held our attention when he showed us a variety of brain scans. We could see the change from the agitated brain to the brain while sleeping, but the most peaceful scan of all was the one that occurred when the person was praying. We were awed at seeing the transformation of the brain from over-activity to being peaceful in prayer.

Our seminar closed with a powerful speaker from the area, Joyce, the founder of a ministry for destitute women. She reminded us that we are in a spiritual battle and encouraged us to be proactive and attack with prayer, fighting for the children of India.

Traveling home I knew this was not the end of MOST Ministries' Suicide Prevention and Depression Awareness seminars in India. Plans were falling into place for a team to return to the United Evangelical Missions in Bangalore the following year.

Many months later, Kalavathy wrote to me expressing her thanks for the seminars. She said that within her school, "teachers are going crazy for the material and many copies are made." I treasured her letter, and the hope that it brought with it.

Over the next few years we sent several teams with many of the same members to India for Suicide Prevention and Depression Awareness seminars, spreading our teachings from the Lutheran Seminary in the very southern tip of Nagercoil, South India, to the northern city of New Delhi.

It was in New Delhi that the local English newspaper reported, on the front page, the prior day's suicides! It was difficult for me to accept this as a regular feature of the newspaper, prominently displayed with the names, ages, and methods of suicide, followed by a brief statement of probable causes. I prayed that someday there would be no need for this section.

While presenting, Linda and Murl discovered that the Indian language and culture was limited in providing vocabulary and opportunities to openly discuss many common feelings. They began to see that the people of India lacked the ability to express some basic emotions. Children needed a way to discuss their feelings of fear, failure and hopelessness.

This discovery became the inspiration for a workbook with interactive lessons where the children could freely discuss their emotions through role-playing, journaling and small group discussions. The focus of this workbook was their emotional and interpersonal development. In thirty lessons, from self-awareness, forgiveness, empathy training, feelings, stress management and problem solving, students would gain scriptural insights to guide them.

With the development of the workbook there also came a change in name. No longer were these seminars called Depression Awareness and Suicide Prevention. They were now called "A Hope and A Future Seminars," inspired by the words from Jeremiah 29:11: "For I know the plans I have for you, declares the Lord, plans to prosper you and not to harm you, plans to give you a hope and a future."

We knew the impact of this new class curriculum was going to be powerful. This workbook would not only give permission to the children to have feelings, but also provide the means to express them, all in a context of the love of Jesus.

With just one team a year, we were limited in how many people we could reach. At this rate I knew it would be a long time before we could expect to share our "Hope" curriculum throughout all of India. We prayed for a national organization that could spread our teachings beyond our reach.

When Campus Crusade of Asia contacted us in 2009 requesting we train their incoming staff, we knew this was God's answer to our prayers. Campus Crusade (Cru) is a large, well-established international

Christian organization, with staff on numerous university campuses. Campus Crusade agreed that this information would complement their ministry well and an arrangement was made to train their staff and give them ownership of our materials.

The opening session was filled with excitement. There were young men and women from Sri Lanka, Pakistan and India who were enthusiastic about the material. We soon learned that many of the attendees had themselves experienced the loss of a friend or family member to suicide. This made it personal. They were ready and eager to learn how to intervene and stop future suicides, bringing an end to the hopelessness and despair that led to these tragedies.

We presented each of the attendees with an EvangeCube, a great visual they could use as they shared their faith on campuses. They were excited to gather in small groups and practice the message with the appropriate twists and turns required to display each new picture on the cube, bringing the story of salvation to life.

A Hindu teacher, attending through a special invitation that Campus Crusade had given to a local school, was fascinated by the message of salvation. Each day she sought me out and spoke to me expressing her gratitude for what she was learning, bowing towards me as a sign of her appreciation and thanking me profusely for her attendance.

Each attendee was encouraged to learn John 3:16: "For God so loved the world that He gave His one and only Son, that whoever believes in Him shall not perish but have eternal life." The Hindu woman surprised us all by standing before the trainees and joyfully explaining her new understanding of this verse, aided by the EvangeCube.

All too soon it was time for the closing ceremony, and with that, the knowledge that our work was done in providing India with suicide prevention training. It was a solemn yet inspiring moment when we passed the master copies to the director of Campus Crusade of Asia

The Hindu woman surprised us all by ...joyfully explaining her new understanding of this verse...

199

I thought back to the day when Jabus shared his concerns for his students. Little did we know the ripples it would cause, and that they would reach far beyond his students! I left the country at peace, my mind filled with the image of the Hindu woman's radiant face embedded in my memory.

Kalavathy and I continued to correspond over the years. It was through our hand written conversations that I began to see how God was using me, as a woman, to inspire other women around the world. Our seminars in Ambur were on the topic of child and teen suicide, but as Kalavathy attended, she was also witnessing God use me, a woman in a role of leadership. In a culture where women have few rights and are expected to be subservient this was an encouraging message for her. After our team left, Kalavathy was inspired to organize a Women's Development Association. Forty-five women—of all social classes and religions—gathered to discuss ways to improve their communities. It was decided that their first and most pressing project was to stop an offensive smell that was coming from the local tannery.

Kalavathy wrote how the women went as a group to the tannery and the owners "were shocked to see all the women together. It was something new for them and of course they stopped the bad smell. In this way we have solved many problems like electricity failure, cleaning the streets, turning an empty lot with debris into a playground for children, etc."

She was the only Christian. The others were Hindu and Muslim, but they came to her for prayers to her God. Kalavathy was their encourager, not only for community affairs but also in their personal lives.

When I returned to India for our final suicide prevention team in 2009, I had the opportunity to visit with Kalavathy. She enthusiastically shared with me her new plans to retire from teaching so that she could volunteer full-time as a school counselor. What a wonderful counselor she would be! Loving, listening and nurturing the children seemed to come naturally for her. The most exciting news that she shared was that there had not been a suicide in their school since the training of the teachers!

Kalavathy has continued to update me on the efforts of the Women's Association Development. In 2015 she shared that the association had fought hard for a piece of property on which they hoped to build a "ration shop," a special store for those under the poverty line where they can receive rice and basic foods from the government. The closest shop is four kilometers away, a difficult distance for the community.

Kalavathy also shared stories of young students she counseled. Several had considered suicide, but chose life because of her intervention and are forever grateful to her. Today, Kalavathy thanks me for my role in her life, but the reality is, she inspires me as she shines the light of Christ through her kindness and compassion for all.

24

Beyond Leprosy

India

I took hold of the woman's outstretched stump as she thanked me; her hand was missing due to her long battle with leprosy. She smiled, studying my face as though it were the first time seeing it. Well, in truth, it was. She was now at the final station of our temporary eyeglass clinic where I had just fitted her with a new pair of eyeglasses, one of our stronger prescriptions.

With the proper correction what was once a blurred image of my face was now transformed into the crisp details of my green eyes and fading red hair. Tears of joy streamed down her face. As she looked, her smile widened. She took in her surroundings, and her face lit up with each new discovery. As I watched the world change before her very eyes, I no longer noticed South India's stifling heat. I didn't see her deformities. I welcomed her touch, knowing that her leprosy, a once deadly disease, was no longer contagious.

It was June 2006. MOST Ministries had been invited to Chennai, India by Youth With a Mission (YWAM) to provide eyeglass clinics for several leper colonies. As Don and I served side by side, nothing seemed to matter—the heat, the amputations, or the poverty. Just this woman and others like her, and the delight they had in their new vision.

Leprosy, also known as Hansen's disease, is a disease often surrounded by negative stigmas. There is no vaccine to prevent leprosy, but thankfully there is medication to stop it as soon as it is diagnosed.

Sadly, those in remote villages often did not receive early treatment. The disease progressed and permanent nerve damage occurred. The result was disfiguring skin sores and nerve damage, which caused deformities in the arms and legs. Many lost fingers, toes or partial limbs.

Although those who receive medical help are no longer contagious, they are still rejected from Indian society. They live in leper colonies separated from the surrounding communities, sent there by law at a time in history when there was no cure. The Indian community, not ready to let go of the centuries-old stigma and fear, forced those with leprosy to live with their families in these colonies.

Health care workers understand that it will take time for society to learn to accept this population. It is hoped that the next generation will be educated to understand that with proper treatment, those with leprosy are no longer a threat. They will then be allowed to live more normal lives at home, in their communities.

Initially, I was surprised by YWAM's request. Wasn't leprosy a disease from the past? I learned that India, with its vast population and remote villages, was one of the last countries struggling to contain the disease. In 2005 India finally reached its lowest rate of new cases.

As Don and I prepared for this team, we wondered how we would react to seeing the severe deformities of those in the colonies. We hoped we would be able to look past the disfigurements to see the person.

We prayed that God would help us and He did. The people were amazing. The tenacity of each individual impressed us as they maneuvered through our clinic, many missing hands or feet, yet managing well and never expecting our sympathy. We had imagined the villagers to be filled with sorrow, yet they were joyous and inspiring. They were grateful for our clinic since the disease often affected their vision.

The tenacity of each individual impressed us as they maneuvered through our clinic...

The previous woman, with no fingers or hands, only arm stubs, amazed me as she effortlessly took her new glasses on and off of her head. This ingenuity was shown repeatedly.

Many scooted along the floor when missing or deformed feet kept them from walking or standing. They were swift and agile; some sat on boards fashioned with wheels to move around.

I was drawn to one very petite woman. She was dressed in a bright yellow and red sari, and had orange powder on her closely shaved head. The powder was turmeric, a spice that is used in India as a cosmetic. She had a distinctly orange glow that is considered attractive for women in India.

I decided to capture her clinic experience on camera by taking a photo of her at each eyeglass station. She was rather sober throughout the testing, but when she received her glasses she immediately broke into a toothless grin. It was obvious she could see clearly! A member of the YWAM team shared her faith with this woman, providing her with Scriptures in Tamil, her language. When she left the clinic she seemed to be glowing from within as well as from the orange turmeric.

After she left I resumed my post at the final eyeglass fitting station of our clinic. A man arrived wearing a pair of his own glasses. The frames were so badly broken that I marveled he could keep them on his face. One stem was missing and the other bent. His creative use of string held them on his face as best it could. It was obvious that he needed these glasses since they were very thick.

What a joy to fit him with not only a new frame but with a perfect prescription. When he removed his old glasses and handed them to me I noticed the badly scratched lenses, no doubt from the many times they fell from his face. I was tempted to ask him if I could have his old pair of glasses to take back home to demonstrate the desperate need for eyeglasses worldwide, but those were his treasure.

He was pleased with his new glasses. He took his hands, with missing fingers, and placed them in the position of prayer as he bowed before me, thanking me for his gift of sight. He left beaming, eager to show his new glasses to his friends and family.

Later that afternoon, I decided to take a break and sit outside. My gaze wandered back to the bustling activity of the eyeglass clinic where my team members were diligently testing and fitting the eager participants. I appreciated how smoothly the clinic was flowing, as each person moved from station to station. I had to smile, because it was not always this way. I remembered the determined thieves of Haiti and the unexpected Kuna Indians of Panama.

As I was reflecting on the past, an elderly man came out of the clinic and sat directly in front of me. He had walked slowly, head bent down, using a stick to guide him, as a blind person would do with a white cane. He carried his new glasses in his hands.

He sat lost in thought and unaware that I was watching him. He had two pair of glasses, one for reading and one for distance. He was fingering the cases to determine which pair to put on for his walk back into the village. After sitting there for a while, he finally settled on his new glasses for distance.

As was his habit, he began the trek home by walking slowly, his head down, still watching and tapping the ground with his stick. After a few steps, he stopped abruptly and lifted his head. He looked around at his newly focused surroundings, at the trees and then down again at the path before him. He then picked up his walking stick, tucked it under his arm and began walking, his head upright. Within a few paces he picked up speed, walking rapidly and confidently out of my sight.

I was grateful to be a silent observer of this man and his gift of sight. It was easy for me to get caught up in the details and logistics of each team. I needed this small reminder of how God was using our teams to affect the lives of individuals. Numbers are impressive, but seeing this drastic transformation of one man was priceless.

We trained the YWAM staff so they could continue providing eyeglasses to the thirty leper colonies in the area. We also provided YWAM with testing equipment, more than a thousand pair of used eyeglasses, and addresses for international warehouses that could continue the supply.

Our time in India also included an evening social event with singing, drama and a dance. It was a unique expression of joy. The dancers

Numbers are impressive, but seeing this drastic transformation of one man was priceless.

didn't have all their fingers or toes, but it didn't prevent them from their joyful expressions of thanksgiving for God's grace.

Again, God amazed me with the lesson that our joy is found in Him, not our circumstances. As I considered my next destination, Kenya, to help the Lutheran church conduct an assessment on the AIDS epidemic, I prayed that I could hold on to the joy of the Lord that these individuals had shown me.

Kenya

25

Numbers and Names

Kenya

They counted on their fingers; naming each person they knew who had died of AIDS in the past year. Sometimes their ten fingers were not enough. In that case, they began around again until all were named.

I listened, hoping for their sake they would cease naming family and friends who were no more. Question number eighty was by far the most difficult of all the questions on our Kenyan AIDS Assessment Tool, "How many people do you know who died of AIDS in the last year?" This answer was not a number, but a listing of loved ones.

It was September 2006, and Don and I were part of a MOST Ministries team serving Kenya. We traveled through cities and rural villages asking preselected individuals questions from our specially designed AIDS Assessment Tool. Reverend David Chuchu from the Evangelical Lutheran Church of Kenya (ELCK) asked MOST Ministries to help assess the region's common attitudes and beliefs regarding AIDS. They also asked if we would provide instructions on good hygiene and nutrition for those with AIDS and those who tested positive for HIV (Human Immunodeficiency Virus), which can lead to AIDS if proper care is not taken.

AIDS is a worldwide epidemic, and the people of Kenya are deeply affected. In 1999 the Kenyan government declared HIV/AIDS a national disaster and public health emergency. According to a 2005 World Health Organization report on Kenya (*Summary Country Profile for*

HIV/AIDS Treatment Scale-Up), over a million people were living with HIV/AIDS and an estimated 1.5 million Kenyans had already died from the disease. It ripped apart families, leaving more than a million children orphaned. Thankfully, the prevalence of new cases appeared to be slowing in 2006.

Our team understood the value of capturing the current views of this syndrome for the Kenyan ministry. This knowledge would allow the ELCK to address specific needs and dispel misconceptions. Don, who had more than twenty years of professional experience in research and test development, and another qualified staff member, designed our questionnaire. It consisted of eighty-six culturally sensitive questions.

Rev. Chuchu preselected each Kenyan who would participate in the one-on-one interviews. These participants represented a cross section of tribes, various social statuses, and geographical districts. There was also a sampling of church leaders, church members, and the community at large.

Our team traveled over 1,000 miles to urban centers and remote tribal villages to meet with the 260 preselected individuals. Seventy were infected with HIV/AIDS.

It was an incredibly challenging undertaking. Days were spent on the bumpy and dusty dirt roads as we traveled to four different church districts. The view out the window was the same in most areas: flat red dirt extending for miles, broken occasionally by Kenya's iconic acacia trees.

As we approached the villages, the streets became congested with men leading donkeys, heavy laden with sacks of grain heading to market. The women wore brightly colored clothing. They used large cotton cloths, called congas, to wrap around themselves in a variety of ways, fashioning dresses and skirts, or strapping children to their backs. They traveled with goods balanced on their heads, as the Haitian women did.

With the help of interpreters, several team members interviewed the chosen Kenyans. While the interviews were taking place, our nurse, nutritionist, and social worker presented seminars for the infected.

They expected to present to small groups, with less than twenty preselected persons with HIV/AIDS at each district, but that was not the case. In the capital city of Nairobi, those without AIDS who were waiting for their interviews interrupted our special nutrition seminar. "Please, please allow us to attend." They pleaded. "We have family and friends who have HIV/AIDS. We *need* nutrition information too." We were happy to include them.

The nutritionist shared how specific food groups were essential to keep the immune system healthy to fight off AIDS. We knew that the suggested foods were available, but often the people were too poor to buy them. In an effort to assist the infected, our MOST Ministries team brought and distributed special seed packets from the ministry HopeSeeds. These packets included several different kinds of vegetables appropriate for the gardening conditions in Kenya.

HopeSeeds was an offshoot of a MOST Ministries team from a 1995 Haiti eyeglass team. The team members returned home, inspired to continue supporting the Haitian people. Mike Mueller, owner of a Florida seed business, became involved. When his congregation sent items to Haiti, Mike began including specially designed seed packets for the Haitians to try. The seeds grew!

Eventually several international ministries asked Mike to research and send his specially-chosen seeds to other impoverished countries. His seeds provided life-giving nourishment around the globe. Mike found his calling! He closed his local seed business and began HopeSeeds, with the mission statement, "Plant a seed, feed a soul."

In Kenya the packets were a big hit as the participants looked forward to growing these essential foods in their own gardens. In addition, several hundred packets were given to the ELCK agriculturalist to develop community gardens, where they could harvest the seeds to save for future crops.

Our larger-than-expected audience remained after the nutritionist finished to hear from the nurse, and then the social worker. Although it was not the small intimate group of persons with HIV/AIDS she had hoped to address, the social worker took advantage of this new audience by engaging them in discussions on the delicate subject of the social impact of living with HIV/AIDS. She guided those with HIV/AIDS from feelings of shame and denial to self-respect and hope. In turn, those with the virus shared their personal struggles with the healthy participants and us.

The message we brought was one of hope. We encouraged those with HIV/AIDS to carry themselves with dignity as children of God. We promised them that God had not abandoned them. They were not being punished. God had given them a compassionate Savior, and that Jesus and the Holy Spirit promised to comfort them.

Those with HIV/AIDS appeared to be more peaceful and confident when they left our presentations.

Those with HIV/AIDS appeared to be more peaceful and confident when they left our presentations. We also encouraged them to be role models of compassion for others and to develop support groups.

As we traveled through the four districts, we began to understand why the infected Kenyans were afraid to reveal their condition to their family members and local communities. Many people wrongly believed that those with HIV/AIDS deserved their illness as a punishment from God for immoral behavior. We were disappointed to see that those living with the virus were not experiencing God's grace from the local church or their community. Many shared in private that they were afraid to tell their family and fellow church members about their condition because they feared they would be condemned and sent away. Although saddened, we were not surprised; these same fears existed in the United States.

One woman told us she was a choir director for a large church and her married daughter had AIDS. She had not revealed her daughter's illness to her congregation because of her position. She worried how the leadership might react. Would they ask her to step down? My heart broke as she quietly whispered her fears to us.

It was obvious that the silence needed to be broken. We did our best to dispel misconceptions and encouraged all Kenyans to be accepting and loving towards anyone with HIV/AIDS, no matter how it was contracted. Indeed, many contracted the illness through intimacy with an unfaithful spouse.

Unfortunately, due to the stigma and the social consequences of having HIV/AIDS, people were choosing not to be tested. We tried to spread the word that there was treatment available to slow the progression when the illness was identified early. Not testing was deadly for themselves and those they might infect! We hoped and prayed that through our discussions and the future efforts of the ELCK, the people would soon understand the need to be tested.

During our presentations I noticed one married couple who diligently wrote down everything. They shared with me that they were both infected. They were very interested in the information about breastfeeding, because they were expecting a baby. It was difficult for them to hear that the virus could pass to their child through the mother's breast milk.

They also listened intently to the session on social impact, as the subjects of shame, stigma, denial, and discrimination were presented. After the session I saw them sitting on the lawn outside of the classroom, discussing our presentation. They had a big decision to make. Would they reveal their condition to their church?

The Sunday following that seminar they stood in front of their large congregation and shared their story, with heads held high. They invited all who were also living with HIV/AIDS to join them as they began a ministry to encourage one another. Many joined, grateful to find encouragement and support. They listened as the couple shared what they had learned in our talks. We were pleased that this brave couple took this giant leap of faith to reveal, rather than conceal, their disease.

A disturbing practice that contributed to the spread of disease in young Kenyan girls was female genital mutilation (FGM). This practice was a cultural norm in many tribal communities. Young girls were initiated into adulthood through a ritual that involved the removal of some or all of the external female genitalia using a razor blade or knife, which was often not sterilized between each ritual cutting. Disease was spread through this traumatic mutilation.

Pain was an important part of the ritual, providing the young girl the opportunity to prove how brave she was. She knew any outward show of pain would diminish her in the eyes of the adults and also her peers. This was an impossible expectation for her to bear.

Unfortunately, there were so many cultural trappings associated with this ritual that the girls, their mothers and grandmothers were reluctant to consider giving up the practice, even as they learned that it spread disease. The women feared that if a young girl did not participate, she would not find a husband within the tribe who would accept her. Her peers would ridicule her, shunning her at school and treating her like a perpetual child. Tribal leaders even misled the young girls into believing they needed this cutting in order to bear children.

Gender issues were at the heart of the problem. We ached for the young girls who were trapped in this deeply entrenched tribal custom. We hoped for a better future as education and knowledge could eventually make a difference. The church had recently begun to educate tribal leaders of the grave dangers of this custom, giving us some hope that the practice may someday cease.

Robert Gutwa, a local Kenyan social worker, shared that the Lutheran church was not only educating the tribes about the dangers of disease from FGM but that they also provided a safe house for girls who ran away to avoid being cut. Mothers who understood the danger would help their daughters leave the village and find refuge in the safe house where they would stay, knowing their tribe would no longer welcome the girls. To take this step was a difficult and brave decision.

After sixteen years of leading teams, I still struggled at the sight of such suffering. My heart broke for the Kenyan HIV/AIDS victims, young and old. My life had become an unusual journey. I was often asked by God to visit some of the darkest of places, seeing and serving people in despair. At times, the suffering was overwhelming, deepening my desire to see change. I knew God could bring hope and light into this darkness; I just needed to *trust Him*.

After spending two long and tedious days tabulating the results of the 260 people who were interviewed, we were able to present a

160-page document to the church leaders with suggestions for future programs of education and ministry.

One recommendation was for the ELCK to provide better care and encouragement for the caregivers of those with HIV/AIDS. The exhausted and overworked family and friends of the ill were in dire need of emotional and physical support.

Rev. Chuchu, a forward thinking man, already had a plan to address this need. Before we departed, he wanted our team to see just one more community. He was developing a ministry for those living with HIV/AIDS in the Kiberia slum, right in the capital city of Nairobi near where we were staying. We didn't have to drive far, no interviews would happen. It would be a quiet walk through a vast slum. Several team members chose not to go, including Don. They had already seen enough suffering.

Rev. Chuchu brought those who chose to go to the Springs of Living Water Church which sat on the edge of a hill overlooking the immense slum. Tin roofs stretched below us for miles. It reminded me of Haiti's Cite Soleil. At first glance it was a bleak picture. Such hopelessness! Rev. Chuchu saw it differently. For him, this was an opportunity to offer the hope of Jesus to thousands. The church was about to open a medical clinic that would eventually serve the 750,000 people living in the slum.

Rev. Chuchu had a special reason for showing me this slum and introducing me to several residents. He hoped MOST Ministries would consider returning with a hospice training team the following year. Rather than teaching medical professionals as we had done in other countries, he wanted us to teach and encourage the weary caregivers who were forced to face the harsh realities of HIV and AIDS as family members battled the disease.

We agreed to return with a MOST Ministries team. How could we say no after seeing such heartbreaking suffering? Wasn't assisting caregivers one of the needs identified for future focus of ELCK? Now God was giving us the opportunity to meet that need.

The Evangelical Lutheran Church of Kenya read and responded to our AIDS Assessment Tool summary. They reached out to each community, addressing the individual needs. Pastors attempted to dispel the common misunderstandings surrounding the illness and encouraged members to have empathy for those who suffered with HIV/AIDS. Many congregations formed support groups.

By changing the atmosphere and removing the shame, Kenyans were more willing to be tested. Once tested, they could receive the life giving treatment provided by the Kenyan Ministry of Health. As a result of these changes in 2016 Rev. Chuchu eagerly shared with MOST Ministries that a number of the people who revealed their illness and were helped with medication "are still alive today!"

26

Care for Caregivers

Kenya

One by one I met the children, quiet and timid. They stared at me with their enormous brown eyes. Little ones clung to Grace, the grandmother, mother, and aunt for a dozen children. Half of them tested positive for HIV/AIDS.

It was 2007, a year after my first visit and I was back in Kiberia, the Kenyan slum. This time it was not for a quiet walk. It was to meet church members who called this slum home. We were there to witness with our eyes, ears, and heart the devastation of the AIDS epidemic firsthand. We wanted to see the current living conditions of the ill, and the struggles of the caregivers, as we prepared for our Palliative Care and Hospice Seminar later that week.

Grace was also infected with the virus. She worried about her future and the children under her care. I sat in her small home and listened as she told me about her challenges. The neighbor's radio blared through the cardboard-thin walls, making it difficult to focus on what the soft-spoken woman said.

While visiting in Grace's neighborhood, we saw one overwhelming challenge for those with AIDS and their caregivers: community pit latrines. These were shared with 100 to 200 families. They were often a long walk from the family home. Grace was closer than most to the latrines, but she feared the day when she would be too weak to make the journey to relieve herself.

It was then that I learned about "flying toilets" from our host, an unusual and unsanitary alternative used by some to avoid the long walk to the latrine. Human feces were deposited directly into plastic bags and then flung high into the air. They landed on hot tin roofs. The bags often exploded on impact, putting the whole neighborhood at risk for more disease.

We left Grace's home to visit Carol. She was able to manage her HIV with medication. With the help of a microloan (a very small amount of money provided by a nonprofit organization), Carol started a small business selling congas, the large brightly colored lengths of cloth used by women as clothing and baby carriers.

We were encouraged as we learned of the many women in this community running small businesses through the help of microloans. The microloans enabled them to purchase the supplies they needed to start up their businesses, like material to sew clothes, or chickens to sell eggs.

Carol graciously invited us into her neatly-kept home, a tin shack with a dirt floor. It was obvious she understood the importance of cleanliness to her fragile condition. The home was as clean and germ free as it could be in this community. It was hard to imagine the extra care she needed to take in her everyday life. I worried for her future.

We were introduced to her three boys and I wondered how they all managed in this ten-foot square space, especially with the lack of privacy. The noise of neighboring radios and conversations continued to distract me.

After several more visits our team was ready to escape back to our clean and quiet housing, but there was one more important stop we needed to make before we made our retreat: the local market place. This would give us a quick glimpse into the availability of nutritious fruits, vegetables, and proteins.

Our presence in the market caused a commotion. We enjoyed good-natured conversation with the vendors; trying to ask questions with only gestures and futile attempts at the local language, Swahili.

As we walked through the market, our occupational therapist, Christian, noted the availability of five-gallon plastic pails with lids and handles. He immediately connected that with the need Grace expressed for a bedside commode. He thought that with a plastic bag inside (which would be properly discarded) and a hole in the lid, this common pail could become a valuable assistive device for the weak and dying.

The next day we gathered at the retreat center with the many church workers and volunteers, some who had traveled great distances. I spoke with one man whose only transportation from his remote village was the back of a truck! He sat in the blazing sun for a day before he was able to connect with a long distance bus to bring him to our location.

The sixty men and women were sent as delegates from their congregations and communities, tasked with returning to train others to care for the ill and dying. All were eager for this training, some having tested positive for HIV themselves.

Our team came prepared to teach all aspects of palliative and hospice care. These were seasoned presenters—a doctor, nurse, social worker, volunteer coordinator, deaconess, occupational therapist and chaplain. Several had been to other countries to teach medical professionals in hospital settings, including Rev. Jim Jasper. Our experienced team tailored their presentations for the needs of caregivers, often family and friends of the ill.

Each day began with worship. The African harmonies and rhythm transported us! A woman next to me sang in a beautiful descant that lifted my spirits. It was difficult to see the worship service end and to come down to earth and focus again on human suffering.

The training topic on one of the days included the revelation of our newly designed commode. Most of the latrines in Kenya are simply cement platforms with a hole in the center, requiring the user to squat to relieve themselves. These are known as a "squatty potty." Because of his concern for Grace and others we met in Kiberia, our creative occupational therapist designed a commode that could be placed by a bedside or carried to a latrine. This inexpensive five gallon plastic bucket with the modified lid was the highlight of the seminar.

Spontaneous applause and cheering came from the participants as they realized the implications of this commode. My friend with the beautiful voice reached over to hug me. With tears streaming down her face, she said, "I will never again be afraid to go and use the latrines. I have fallen three times because of the pain in my knees when I squat. Praise God! He has saved me from my fear of this happening again."

We wept together. Her tears were for joy, but mine were for her suffering.

One afternoon a special training session was held for the pastors in attendance, led by Rev. Jasper. This session focused on the spiritual nature of man and man's suffering. Thus began the formation of a close bond as these men could often be seen gathering together during breaks to continue their discussions with him. As I saw these pastors with their strong desire to minister to the dying, I recalled the assessment team and the fear that some AIDS suffering church members had of being condemned by their pastors. I knew that these men would return to their congregations offering compassion to all.

Praise God! He has saved me from my fear...

As we prepared for this team, we had considered the needs of the children. Too many had experienced the death of one or both of their parents. We decided to create a hands-on booklet just for them. After our arrival in Kenya, we expanded the idea with input from many of the participants. The newly created fourteen-page booklet encouraged children to record their feelings of loneliness, anger, fear, and confusion as well as special times with their parent. Blank pages were included, with suggestions for them to picture their emotions and memories. We included the text from Psalm twenty-three for those who could read

This became a treasured resource that would be translated into the local languages for hundreds of children. Entitled "My Journey," it would preserve the precious memories of loved ones and help children to process their grief.

The room was alive with the intensity of the teaching and the eagerness of the participants to fully comprehend the presentations. Pain management and the types of medication available for treatment were presented by Dr. Vilnis Sosars. Deaconess Mary Anne stressed the need for forgiveness and reconciliation among family members. She also talked about what to expect in the process of grieving. Jan, the social worker, stressed the social and emotional needs of the patient and the family.

Mary, my brother Gordon's daughter, joined us on this team as our nurse. She demonstrated practical skills, such as how to transfer a patient from one position to another without injuring the caregiver. Leah, a volunteer coordinator, instructed delegates on how to organize volunteers within their churches, as they hoped to engage their members in the care of the dying.

The delegates listened intently and wrote detailed notes in their syllabuses. Each evening, they reviewed the day's materials.

On the last day our host, Rev. Chuchu, presented an official plan of action. We had trained the trainers, and now they were to return to their congregations empowered to implement what they had learned. Our 170-page syllabus was the textbook that would equip them in their mission to train.

At our closing ceremony I was swept up in God's power and grace. For me, it was the end of my time in Kenya. For the new palliative care workers, the closing ceremony signaled the beginning of their new ministry to provide compassion and dignity for the dying.

The message was the same in Latvia, Kyrgyzstan, China, India, and Kenya. God has compassion for those who are nearing the end of their lives. He calls us to reach out with His love and grace. Throughout the years the compelling words of the apostle Paul encouraged my team members and me to press on: "Let us not become weary in doing good, for at the proper time we will reap a harvest if we do not give up." (Galatians 6:9). Together we have seen a great harvest!

Back Home

27

It Starts with You

"Did you know that it was after I went on a MOST Ministries team to Latvia at the age of sixteen that I felt called to a life of ministry?" asked the chaplain of Concordia University, Ann Arbor. "That was the catalyst that began my journey to serve full-time. Thank you!"

We had not known. His words surprised and inspired Don and me. The chaplain's words echoed in my mind for weeks. *"Did you know...?"*

It was 2014, and much had changed for us. In 2006 I stepped down from my role as Executive Director of MOST Ministries. At the age of 68 after 16 years of leading the ministry, Don and I agreed that it was time. Although we were ready to slow down, we were not ready to say our goodbyes to MOST Ministries. It is a part of who we are. I was grateful to be able to continue as a team leader and we both remained on the board of directors. The ministry was strong and operated smoothly without our daily input, giving us a clear sign that it was God's ministry, not ours.

In 2007 we left our home of forty years and moved to Wheaton, Illinois to be near family. I continued to lead teams, mostly to South and Central America. I also took teams to new countries, such as Israel, where we served Palestinian Christians in Bethlehem. Don continued to support the eyeglass ministry from home, exploring new possibilities.

The year 2014 was special. It marked the 25th anniversary of our first team to Haiti. MOST Ministries held several events to commemorate the occasion. During this year of celebration and reflection Don and I spent time pulling out old photo albums and journals and reliving our amazing adventures together. Each photograph brought forth a flood of memories as we viewed the faces of team members and those we served.

When we considered all that God had done through the ministry it was almost overwhelming. We frequently heard new stories of rippling effects from MOST Ministries team members, like the university chaplain who found his calling at a young age through a team to Latvia. Don and I knew that the ripples would continue as this chaplain mentored college students who in turn might respond to God's calling, serving Him in their own unique way.

It is like a continuous rainfall, Lord, I thought to myself, *each drop creating more and more ripples! You rain Your blessings down through Your faithful people, and in turn the ripples of their faithful service create more willing hearts to serve, causing more blessings to fall. How great You are!*

As Don and I reminisced, I recalled my early uncertainties while leading MOST Ministries. Feeling that I was not fully qualified for what He had called me to do, I had often asked God, *"Why me?"* At first I thought that I was called because God asked others before me, but they had not responded. As a result He asked me, the less qualified option. I can see now that I was **not** His person of last resort. God used my life experiences to mold me into the person He wanted me to become, preparing me for His purposes.

As 2014 came to a close, we were astounded to hear the final numbers for the first quarter century of service. MOST Ministries had sent out over 400 teams with over 5,000 team members. Teams had been sent to forty-eight different countries and served over 180,000 people! We were filled with awe.

The statistics for our eyeglass teams were particularly impressive. Of those served, 114,000 received eyeglasses. Thousands more continue to be given eyeglasses through established eyeglass clinics trained by MOST Ministries' teams in countries like Latvia and Kyrgyzstan. Eileen has continued her eBay sales of used glasses, selling to over sixty countries! The profits average $17,000 a year, contributing greatly toward the costs of the eyeglass ministry!

To add to the list of God's goodness and ministry growth was the fact that MOST Ministries was now operating out of its own building, purchased in 2012. We finally had the space needed for storage, offices and volunteers.

When Don and I made the decision in 1992 for me to work full-time organizing short-term mission teams, we never imagined that two decades later the ministry would be fully staffed, sending out an average of twenty-eight teams a year, and owning its own building. This was clearly beyond our sight!

The year 2015 began with excitement as the ministry turned its attention from the past to the future. All twenty team leaders, including me, gathered in January for the annual MOST Ministries team leader retreat.

Our retreat theme was "It Starts with You." The inspiring and thought-provoking statement encouraged me, at the age of seventy-seven, to wonder what God still had in store for me. It also made me think of the past. I thought of the many individuals of whom I could say, *"It started with them"*: Rev. Arboret, Dr. Sosars, Jabus, Kalavathy and numerous others.

As I looked around the room at the faces of those gathered, many of them decades younger than myself, I thought of the future and wondered, *what unique passions and desires has God placed on their hearts? Who will they serve?*

Our retreat began with updates on the ministry's most recent focus, clean water teams in Nicaragua. They were a huge success. Filtration systems previously installed by MOST Ministries' teams had resulted in a decrease in "belly pains" and families reported significantly fewer missed days of school and work due to illness. Plans were put in place to expand and promote these clean water teams.

Our team administrator shared her plans to explore how MOST Ministries could help nationals address and intervene in the horrible practice of human trafficking. I admired her drive to tackle this daunting international problem.

During a time of devotion the retreat leader led us in singing the hymn "Here I Am Lord" by Dan Schutte. It was emotional for me to join in as I remembered many tender moments with the Lord in the past when I had sung and prayed these very words from the refrain.

> Here I am Lord, Is it I Lord?
> I have heard you calling in the night
> I will go Lord, If you lead me
> I will hold your people in my heart.

The words rang like an anthem for thousands of team members and volunteers who were holding His people in their hearts, having responded to His call over the past quarter century and for all who eagerly say "Here I am, Lord!"

God knew what the impact would be on me and others long ago when I heard His call and responded to that simple plea on a video. God did not care that I came from a family that society rejected, that I had once denied His existence or that I would continue to struggle to trust Him. God called me, flaws and all, just as He calls each of us and says *"It Starts With You!"*

Epilogue

Epilogue

A Father's Blessing

As I was sorting through past ministry documents, a handwritten letter in my father's familiar penmanship caught my attention. I was surprised to see this personal correspondence, written decades earlier, mixed in with my ministry notes. *Why was it there?* Intrigued, I stopped what I was doing and gave this weathered piece of paper my full attention.

Both of my parents had long since passed away. I missed my mother dearly, and lovingly thought of the day we would be reunited in Heaven, but I rarely thought of my late father.

The letter had been written during my father's retirement, at a time when he had come to know the Lord as his Savior. I had been pleased that he was showing signs of a growing faith, but I remained very guarded, unwilling to risk the hope of a healthy father-daughter relationship.

As I studied the letter I slowly began to remember the circumstances under which this correspondence had been written. Don and I had attended a Christian conference in the 1980's and a presenter had spoken on improving relationships with parents. He had suggested sending a letter asking our parents what their goals and wishes were for our lives. I chose to act on this recommendation, and sent my father a letter. I was doubtful he would reply. But he did and his words, written with his fourth grade education, were surprisingly wonderful. His goals and wishes for me were:

For a long and happy life with her family and have good Christian children and have a God loving home and help with the church work and may the Lord Bless in this. And may she have a long and healthy life and do to others as she would do for herself and may she have good health to do the Lord's work. I hope this will be her goal in all times. June 1986

I sat on my couch and read the letter, over and over. *Why had I discovered this long forgotten note on this day and at this time?* I wondered, *Lord, is this from you?* At first, I read it with the same cool and distant emotional response as when I had first received it. These words did not fit the man that I knew. The little girl inside of me found these kind words hard to accept. In fact, I did not want to accept them. I wanted to be distant, but the words would not go away.

For days I pondered them. I had to admit; they seemed amazing, loving and inspiring. When I shared them with others, who knew of my past, they marveled and rejoiced, seeing how God's hand had been at work in my father's life. It was like the happy resolution to a movie; the antagonist had changed his ways.

Why then had I not played my part? I wondered. *Why had I not opened my arms and received him, rejoicing together and sharing our love for the Lord?* I was even more troubled as I questioned my current emotions. *Why am I not rejoicing now? Why is my heart still so hard?* Days led to weeks and I still had no answer.

Slowly, I began to understand. I was trapped and unable to see my father through adult eyes. When I thought of him, I was instantly transformed into the little girl who lived in fear. In my child's mind, life was black and white with clear rights and wrongs and my father had been wrong. All wrong.

God was helping me to see there were other points of view. Yes, my father made mistakes, but he had also worked two jobs to put food on the table and keep a roof over my head. I tried to understand the stress he must have been under as an uneducated man trying to provide for his family.

I needed to offer my father grace and forgiveness. With tears in my eyes, I did.

After I dared to pull away the dark curtain of my childhood, I was convicted of my own more recent errors. I had been wrong as an adult to not acknowledge the changes in my father. With a wave of guilt I felt the more recent remorse that I was trying to hide. I knew that I should have attempted to restore our relationship once he began to change, but I had not! My unresolved childhood pain had created a barrier.

My heart was heavy as I acknowledged my own wrongs, the pain and guilt overwhelming, but God is good and gracious and reminded me of the prophet Nehemiah's encouraging words: "You are a God of forgiveness, gracious and slow to become angry and rich in unfailing love" (Nehemiah 9:17).

After seeking forgiveness, a new peace filled my soul. I dried my eyes and took a deep breath, feeling relief and renewed joy. I reread the long forgotten blessing, and saw my father anew. The curtain had been opened and God shown His light deep into my soul and for the first time ever, I found myself rejoicing over the idea of someday being reunited with my earthly father in Heaven!

I now see my father's handwritten wishes like a special blessing and prayer spoken over me so many years ago. What my father asked of the Lord has come about in my life. I have had a long and healthy life, raised a Godly family and I made it my goal to serve others and do the Lord's work.

Thank you, Dad.

Macau Buddhist Temple

Burning of paper clothes for ancestor in Hell fills the air with ash and soot.

A sacrifice to Buddha: a sack of boiled potatoes and a cooked duck.

Buddha and lesser gods.
Their arms are made of stone as well as their hearts.

Praying on Site with Insight

Prayer walking at Tiananmen Square.
Forbidden City is in the background.

Many people were baptized into the Christian
faith at the Three Self Church in Beijing.

Abandoned

A formal Chinese welcoming for
Dr. Sosars, Gayle, Pastor Mike, and Pat, RN.

Listening intently but not understanding
"Dying with Dignity".

She beamed with delight when she could see clearly.
Permission was granted to build a new church as
a result of this eyeglass clinic.

Chinese pastor beaming after learning that he
received permission to expand his church building—
all because our team had chosen to worship
with him!

Silent Witness

Long lines waiting for registration in the Muslim village where no verbal witness was permitted.

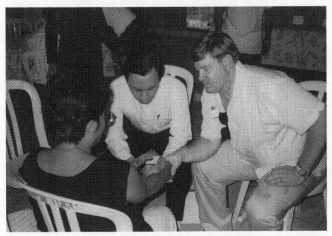

Lines also formed for prayer in villages where witnessing was encouraged. Pastor Mike responds to personal prayer requests.

We Act in Faith

Open air chapel

Dr. Joel strolling with patient on the grounds of Bethesda Hospital.

Dr. Sosars presenting the hospice philosophy.

Women's Ministry in India

Special bonding time in the session for pastors' wives.

Dot and Pastor Udaynesson present Tamil Bibles to all the women who attended the women's ministry sessions.

India Leper Colony

He arrived using his stick as a cane, looking down, walking slowly because of limited vision.
He left carrying his stick and moving quickly towards his home.

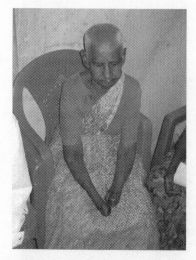

She was shy during testing until she received her sun glasses.

She impressed us by effortlessly taking her glasses on and off despite her stumps.